DATE DUE

BE 2'02			

DEMCO 38-296

tWO
THOUSAND
YEARS

To Joyce, who made it possible

Two
THOUSAND
YEARS

The First Millennium:
The Birth of Christianity to the Crusades

Peter Partner

With a foreword by Melvyn Bragg

GRANADA
MEDIA

With thanks to Richard Thomson and Simon Cherry

First published in Great Britain in 1999
By Granada Media, an imprint of André Deutsch Limited,
in association with Granada Media Group.
76 Dean Street
London
W1V 5HA
www.vci.co.uk

ISBN 0 233 99665 6
Editorial Cover(to)Cover a.t.e.
Picture research by Sophie Seebohm
Book design © Design/Section
2000 Years titles logo © Hobbins Sides
Front cover images 3,4,7, 11, 14,15,16 & 17 © 1998 PhotoDisc, Inc

Printed in the UK by Butler & Tanner, London, and Frome, Somerset

1 3 5 7 9 10 8 6 4 2

CONTENTS

FOREWORD

I owe Christianity a debt, and so, I believe, does the world we have lived in for the last 2000 years. Much of what is best in that duo-millennial span has been inspired by the man who inspired the faith which took his name.

The Alaham Monastery, Turkey

But Christianity also owes me an explanation. As it does to so many others: for the bigotry, the wickedness, the inhumanity and the wilful ignorance which has also characterized much of its 'history'. Its force and extraordinary persistence have informed 'the best of times and the worst of times', from the manger in Bethlehem to the gas chambers of Auschwitz.

It has been the pivot of the argument in matters of morality as it has been in questions of immorality, divine intervention and the source and nature of truth. Music, architecture, art and society have risen to show off the powers of Christianity while states, monarchs, despots, villains and all the variety of the corrupt have used and abused its messages and its meanings throughout the centuries.

It has made secular wars more senseless by its involvement and hopeless conditions hopeful by its devotion. Literature has flourished under its example – indeed the Bible is probably the most influential of all books of literature – but literature has also been censored. Science was sent into outer darkness for centuries, clawing its way back despite persecution and terror. Yet science, despite seeming the ultimate challenge to Christianity, has recently presented it with the Big Bang theory, which appears to dovetail so happily with the Book of Genesis.

Over two thousand years, where there has been slavery, where there has been sacrifice, where there has been enlightenment, where there has been suppression, for richer and poorer until death and beyond Christianity has wedded itself to civilizations and through them it has flooded the world more forcefully and with more perseverence than any other religion.

In more pious days, all of a couple of generations ago, Hollywood called a film about Jesus Christ *The Greatest Story Ever Told*. We would not use that phrase now, but in their epic populist boldness, ironically the Jewish men who ran the world's dream factory knew what they were dealing with.

More sensitive or more politic or less Christ-struck today, we might tend to be apologetic about the Greatest Story. When I suggested we make twenty television programmes of one hour each on the history of Christianity century by century, coupled with discussions arising from some of the engrossing and vivid and perennially relevant issues engendered by the complex penetrations made into the minds and estates of humankind by Christianity, I was aware, almost at the same moment as the simple notion struck, that there would be questions raised on all sides – partly because other religions and other non-religions might feel affronted or even diminished by the implications of non-inclusion in what for British television is a huge commitment.

But this is the year which marks the 2000th anniversary of the birth of Jesus Christ, whose ministry and Church have marked the centuries indelibly and whose presence is still global, active and powerful. Of course there are similar series to be made about Judaism, about Islam, about Buddhism, Hinduism, Confucianism and about more secular beliefs and systems – Marxism, Capitalism, monarchism, tyranny, paganism, various shades of anthems and so they go on and on into the night of the twentieth century, arriving finally at its monstrous Gemini – Fascism and Communism and their nightmare progeny Hitler and Stalin, Mao, Pol Pot and all their ideological offspring. And some of this too is part of the Christian story, some of them drawing strength from Christianity, alas, and some of them using Christianity as a necessary opposition.

Maybe all the work we do is some form of paying debts. I began regular churchgoing – Church of England – in the early 1940s. In 1945 I joined the local choir of St Mary's in Wigton, Cumbria, and sang Sunday after Sunday, two or three times a day for twelve years.

I still know prayers and psalms, hymns and collects by heart, still hear the music, remember snatches of the sermons, can feel the crushing, holy silence, live with the guilt which if not engineered by religion was certainly stirred and spiced by it, still think the Sermon on the Mount is the most radical manifesto ever delivered, still clutch at God at unexpected moments and still have the fundamental doubts about His existence which I began to experience at the age of about sixteen or seventeen.

It is difficult perhaps for younger generations to imagine a place known so well and often hated so firmly by so many of us until recently. The place I speak of is Sunday. A place of suffocated silence and closures. A place where casual blasphemy outside the male workforce was absolutely forbidden; a place in which a small town such as my own in the north of England with a population of about 5,000, could support more than a dozen flourishing churches of different denominations. A place where the churches stood as pillars of the community and centres for the stern and innocent leisure which was most of our public ration of fun.

There is also personal anger. Did we have to be driven so unremittingly with that intransigent image of utter perfection which will never leave us and still haunts to torment us? The forgiveness of the Father could not really cancel that out because we were never good enough to earn it. Did guilt have to be so remorselessly cultivated until all pleasure became stolen – sweeter perhaps for that but also corroded by the sense of sin in which we became Olympic contenders? Were the contradictions never to be pointed out until we ourselves dared raise them, only to be pitied and dismissed? Simple questions never addressed until we had to shut them into the void. How did Cain and Abel get children? Why did Christianity support evil people? What does eternal life mean? Where exactly is the soul? Answers came there none.

So this twenty-hour enterprise for me has been one which has returned to open up old pathways to see where they now lead, wondering why and how they once dominated my life entirely, spiritually – if one can claim that – and intellectually – an even more tenuous claim for the religiously saturated boy I was then, fired to be a missionary and earnest beyond embarrassment even when a teenager kneeling by the bed, in prayers before sleep.

© Peter Willi/Bridgeman Art Library, London

The Borghese gladiator

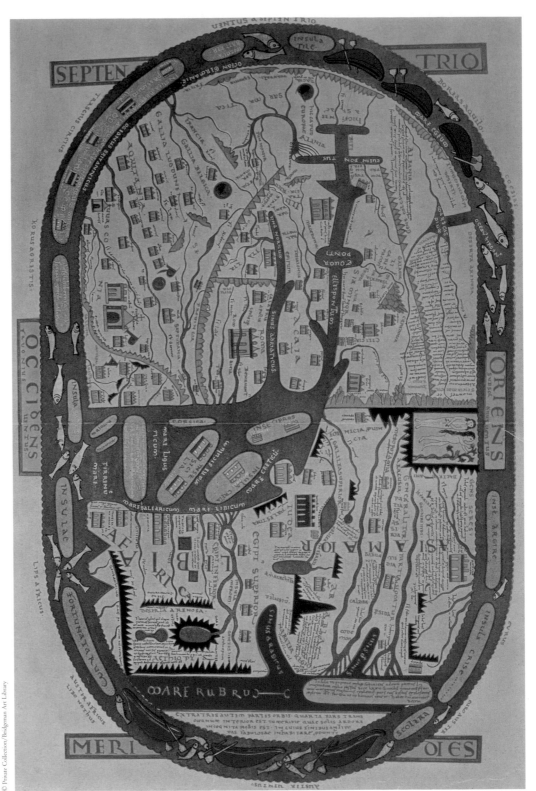

Beatus Mappamundi, c. eighth century

On the broadest level, what meets you when you return to the Gospels, which are the burning core of Christianity, and when you scan the history of two thousand Christian years, is the clamour of events, the violence of the arguments and the men, men, men whose furies drove them for and against the teaching of the gentle rabbi on the shores of Galilee.

The voice of Constantine is there with his earth-changing dream of victory in battle, which made him convert to Christianity. He took care not to do it until the very end of his life, but during the greater part of his reign he dismantled almost four centuries of persecution, slaughter and intolerance. By the end of the fourth century the Emperor Theodosius was forced to beg mercy from Bishop Ambrose of Milan, who had been appalled by the massacres at Thessalonika and excommunicated him. Though the State would use the Church whenever it could and abuse it and distort the teachings and the purpose of its founder, yet the journey of the outlawed sect which began in Judea and persisted for centuries, finally displacing all other gods in the greatest empire on earth, is an astounding tale.

So too is the story of Charlemagne, 400 years after Constantine, when, inspired by English missionaries, he conquered pagan tribes and forcibly converted them to Christianity, thus re-establishing but more emphatically, the empire. But this time it was not the Roman Empire but the Holy Roman Empire. He also took on the mantle of teacher, and book production and the invention of a new more legible system of writing thrived under his rule, which reached a climax on Christmas Day 800, when Pope Leo III crowned him as the first Holy Roman Emperor.

The success of Christianity in the worldly sphere was paralleled by its influence among the unworldly. In fact it scaled new pinnacles of self-abnegation – literally in the case of the hero of the desert coenobites, Simeon Stylites, who became a venerated figure by living on the top of a pillar for thirty-eight years. The Celtic saints emanating from Ireland – in which St Patrick, it was said, sowed seeds which yielded the rich harvest of holy men and women – spread across the islands of Britain and east on to the mainland of Europe, driven there by their emulation of the Acts of the Apostles.

Christianity produced the Gospels – the life and teachings of Christ – whose influence will bear comparison to anything written anywhere ever. It has inspired philosophers and commentators, the most dynamic of whom, Saint Augustine of Hippo, still speaks to the human and the spiritual condition today.

With its written Gospels, its moral system, its equal invitation to all to believe and so to join, its promise of eternal life and its remarkable tenacity, Christianity in its first thousand years came out of insignificance, through the most fearful oppression of centuries, to ride successive waves of barbarism and often equally worrying patronage, and in that first thousand years entered into every structure of life in the increasing number of people and tribes it embraced. It could be ludicrous as it showed in 897 at the Cadaver Synod, in which the corpse of Pope Formosus was put on trial, mutilated and hurled into the Tiber. It could be swept into the worst of millenarianism, as when Emperor Otto III had his ancestor Charlemagne disinterred and moved to his court in Rome to wait for the world to end in the year 1000.

But in those first thousand years, it had become a force which would capture emperors and captivate the humblest individual, be seen as salvation for the peasant and fulfilment for the ruler. The first millennium passed and the world did not come to an end – and neither did Christianity.

Melvyn Bragg, 1999

1

THE BIRTH OF CHRISTIANITY

Jesus of Nazareth was a Jewish charismatic healer, exorcist and religious teacher. That may be a bald statement, but reliable information about him is very scarce, and in human terms it must do. It is extremely hard to see what connections exist between this Jewish holy man of a remote past, and the complex stories of human desires, failures and ideals that fill the rest of this book. Some connections do exist, although they constantly slip out of the grasp of even the most learned. About human salvation, which has very little to do with history books, and perhaps not much to do with theology manuals, Jesus of Nazareth has in the reckoning of many wise persons a great deal, perhaps everything, to say to us.

Jesus was executed by the Roman government in Jerusalem, probably in or close to the year 36 of the Common Era, at the time of the Passover feast. He and his closest followers, along with large numbers of other Jews, had gone to sacrifice at the Temple prior to a private celebration of the appropriate religious acts. Jesus had perhaps made an earlier public entry into the city, which could have been understood as a form of political provocation. Before the feast he created a disorder in the Temple: whether his arrest by the Jewish Temple authorities was a result of his actions in the sacred area on this occasion, or whether they had already determined to arrest him at some earlier point, is not known.

Evidence about the life and career of Jesus is very patchy. This is not surprising, because we are dealing with someone whose political importance as a Jewish religious teacher was so slight in his lifetime that we would know hardly anything about him if we excluded the evidence contained in the writings of his early followers. Evidence about his last days is also obscured because those responsible for the main Gospel texts wished to avoid suggesting that he constituted a security risk for the Roman rulers. In exonerating him they were right in the sense that it is unlikely that Jesus belonged to one of the terrorist Zealot groups that conspired against Roman rule. But Jesus proclaimed a personal

Left: A coarse stone mosaic of Christ dating from the third century.

prophetic mission, referred to the early establishment of a 'kingdom', and violently denounced the priests (established by the Roman government) in charge of the holiest religious site. Such a person was bound to be thought an extremist who constituted an appreciable security risk, both for the priestly establishment and for the Roman authorities that stood behind it.

The high priest of Jerusalem must have brought grave religious charges against Jesus, although whether this was in a religious court with the legal jurisdiction to pronounce sentence is doubtful. If reports are accurate, Jesus rent his own priestly garments during the course of the examination, which would have been a drastic symbolic act. But the subsequent Roman capital condemnation of the accused man was on the political, not religious, grounds that he had claimed to be in some way 'King of the Jews'. This was what was written on the crime or charge sheet that was posted above him at the head of the cross. A comparable situation, due to a crisis of some other form of religious extremism, Jewish, Christian or Muslim, is quite conceivable in the Jerusalem of today.

Crucifixion, the terrible death inflicted in an almost casual way upon Jesus, was not in the least unusual — and before we condescendingly add 'for its time', it would be as well to remember that equally terrible forms of death have been imposed upon huge numbers of people within the lifetimes of persons alive today. But the demeaning, humiliating nature of a punishment used in the ancient world for the lowest criminals or the most despised political enemies has to be emphasized to modern people. Someone in the early period of Roman Christianity, who wanted to ridicule the Christians, made a cruel caricature of a crucified man with the head of an ass.

Jesus in History

One of the first people to inquire into the historical Jesus was the Emperor Domitian (AD 51–96), who is said to have sent police investigators to Galilee to interrogate his surviving family, about fifty years after Jesus' death. They were found to be hard-handed peasants getting subsistence from a smallholding, and were released without charge. However, if Domitian, who was worried about the refusal of the Jesus sect to acknowledge his own divinity and that of the other gods, sent a mission of this sort, it tells us that the sect was no longer totally obscure. If the imperial government bothered to pull in the great-nephews of Jesus for questioning so soon after his death, it shows how quickly judgements about his political significance had changed in the realist world of the Roman Empire.

Even the dates of the birth and death of Jesus are uncertain. It is unlikely that he was born almost exactly two thousand years ago, in the year commonly called the first year of Our Lord (AD 1). A rather rough-and-ready judgement was made, some five centuries after Jesus, concerning the date then chosen for the year to be treated as the first 'year of the Incarnation of Our Lord'. For reasons of convenience, this date for the beginning of the Christian (or Common) Era is the one that is still commonly used, although Jesus was probably born several years before it. The date of 4 'B[efore] C[hrist]' has often been put forward as that of the birth of Jesus. But some have argued for an even earlier date. The doubt about the birth date, which was certainly not at the time of the pagan feasts of the Winter Solstice, means that the Christian millennium has very probably already passed. This is a conclusion that may worry some people, and comfort others. The date of the death of Jesus is just as hard to establish. It probably (but not quite certainly) took place between AD 26 and AD 36, the period during which Pontius Pilate was Roman prefect of Judaea. Many scholars prefer the period between AD 30 and AD 36.

© AKG London

Above: A third-century Roman graffito caricatures the crucifixion. Christ is shown with the head of an ass; the inscription reads 'Alexamanos prays to his God'.

Below: Domitian, shown on a golden coin, became Roman Emperor in AD 81. He launched inquiries into Jesus' family, indicating that the Roman leadership had begun to take the new Christian sect seriously.

© Private Collection/Bridgeman Art Library, London

There is very little indication that Jesus expected anything like Christianity to happen. Nothing in his career or sayings, if we exclude things that seem to have been invented or changed to fit in with doctrines that followed his death, clearly authorizes us to think that he intended to challenge the whole fabric of Jewish practice and belief, in spite of his conviction that the orthodox Judaism of his time had failed. That Jesus thought that he stood in a special relationship to God is certain, and followed directly from his prophetic mission. That he thought of this relationship in terms comparable to those used about him in later Christian definitions of faith is very unlikely, especially if we accept the full humanity and the purely human consciousness that these same definitions assert.

But, in spite of later adjustments and additions to what was written about Jesus in the Gospels, a core of his reported teaching and action refers to a great Jewish teacher who had a clear idea of what he stood for and what he was doing. That cannot be explained by the needs of a later Christian community whose aims lay essentially among the Gentiles. Jesus' teaching was a subtle blend of rigorism, or strictly judged conduct (especially evident in the precepts about sexual relations) and flexible, humane advice (expressed very often in parables). Behind it lay a profound conviction of his own authority to proclaim his mission, and of an imminent, divine judgement on Jewish society (typically expressed in the eschatalogical prophecy of the overthrow of the Temple).

Alexander's Legacy: Hellenization

For well over two centuries, Jewish society in Palestine had been subject to intense Greek, or subsequently Graeco-Roman, cultural pressure, a process known as Hellenization. Two Greek dynasties, the Ptolemaic and the Seleucid, had contested for rule in Palestine during the third century BC. After the Seleucid victory, the new rulers of Syria-Palestine had made a most determined effort to achieve a complete Hellenization of the elites of the area, even to the extent of changing, for a short time, the entire pattern of the worship in the Temple in Jerusalem. Worship of Zeus, the head of the Greek pantheon, was substituted for that of the Old Testament God, Yahweh, and circumcision was abandoned.

Nor was this only a local trend; the Hellenization of the Middle East was part of a drift that affected the whole huge area of Alexander the Great's conquests in the fourth century BC. Large numbers of Jews were dispersed over a vast Middle Eastern and Mediterranean zone, partly because of forced emigrations, partly because of economic pressures. Jewish culture and teaching continued to be marked by strong scripturalism, insistence on the fulfilment of precise dietary and ritualistic practices, of which circumcision of males was the most important, and the conviction that salvation history was to be worked out by and for the Jewish people alone. But the Jews went a long way towards interpreting their own religious tradition in Greek terms. The extent of their cultural acclimatization may be judged from the fact that the Greek 'Septuagint' – sacred writings made in Egypt in the third and second centuries BC – are thought to be guides as valuable to the various critical revisions of the texts as the existing (but largely later) Hebrew versions themselves, not excluding Biblical texts among the Dead Sea Scrolls.

There was fierce and successful resistance to the direct Hellenization of Jewish religion. It led to the liberation wars waged by the family of Judas Maccabaeus, and to the emergence from that family of the Hasmonean dynasty of which Herod the Great was a late and unpopular member. This did not achieve the triumph of Jewish separatism in Palestine: what had begun as a Jewish revolutionary movement became in the end a Roman satellite government. In spite of Roman protection of the

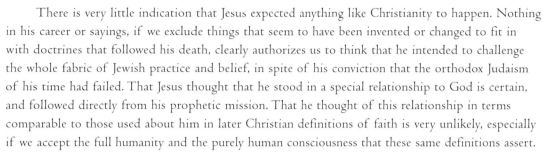

Above: An ivory carving dating from c. AD 420 shows the crucifixion of Christ. Crucifixion was considered a particularly demeaning form of execution, much favoured by the Romans.

Above: Zeus, having adopted the form of a bull, abducts Europa. During the period of intense Hellenization, worship of Zeus, king of the Greek gods, replaced that of Yahweh in Jerusalem.

approved Jewish Temple worship, the predominance of Greek culture in Roman Imperial Asia was as undeniable in Jesus' day as the predominance of American electronic culture is in our own. Renewed Jewish resistance was manifested in Zealot terrorism, but their rebellion collapsed in AD 70, and was punished by the destruction of the Temple of Jerusalem by the Roman Emperor Titus (AD 39–81). These were the brutal facts of Roman political domination. However, Graeco-Roman cultural influence was more subtle and insidious than military might, and profoundly affected the Jewish religious elites. By the time of Jesus, it was an influence already centuries old.

Jesus in Context

Jesus came from Galilee, a rural though prosperous area of Palestine in which Greek cultural presence was at its lowest. It was not entirely absent in Capernaum, where Jesus is known to have taught and worked. But it was much stronger in Sepphoris. The city of Sepphoris was very near his home village of Nazareth, but his presence in the former place is not attested. This may have a sort of negative political significance: at the minimum it meant that he did not think the city a suitable place for the exercise of his ministry. Galilee was a notorious stronghold of Jewish, anti-Roman nationalism and – in Roman terms – terrorism. The Galilean reputation may have contributed to the feelings of political insecurity that marked the Jewish and Roman official response, when Jesus came to the attention of the authorities at the end of his life.

But whatever his tactics may have been in avoiding a city such as Sepphoris, Jesus' ministry was certainly directed to Hellenized or partly Hellenized Jews no less than to those who were not, as is evident from the Greek language of the Gospels themselves. At Ephesus, St Paul and his mission are said to have received into their congregation a highly educated Alexandrine Jew called Apollos. He was a trained Greek orator who had, years earlier, received the rite of baptism of the Evangelist John, most probably from Jesus himself.

Besides being a charismatic healer and exorcist, Jesus was also a prophet who denounced the sins and inadequacies of the leaders of the people. He preached, mostly through allusion and parable, 'the kingdom of heaven', which was something between an immediately available new moral order in which men and women could live in a quite new, God-inspired way, and an imminent

Left: A detail from the Arch of Titus, showing Romans removing the menorah – the Jewish seven-branched candlestick – from the Temple of Jerusalem.

Above: Lake Genezareth, Galilee.

Below: Countryside around Nazareth. Little is known with certainty about Jesus, but he came from Galilee, a main centre of Judaism. His home village was Nazareth.

Right: A stone relief showing Jesus raising from a death-like sleep the 12-year-old daughter of Jairus, a Jewish merchant. This was one of the miracles of healing performed by Jesus and described in the Gospels.

divine judgement. In all these functions he had Jewish contemporaries or near-contemporaries whose paths were in some ways similar or comparable, although none who is known to have united with healing and prophecy, as he did, the gift of convincing all sorts of men and women how they ought to live their lives.

The Essene Sect

There was a kind of social openness, especially to Gentiles, about the way Jesus preached his message, that may have been characteristic of the wandering exorcist healers. He differed deeply from various inward-looking religious groups such as the contemporary one of the Essenes. This was a sect that emphasized above all the apartness of the chosen few of a chosen people, who lived in small, sequestered groups, and were convinced of their own exclusive God-given and race-conferred knowledge of Jewish salvation history.

There are no obvious points of contact between the kind of prophecies attributed to Jesus and those found in the writings of the Essenes. The central Essene doctrines relate to the unnamed 'Teacher of Righteousness', who was betrayed by 'the Liar' or 'the Wicked Priest', at some time before the Romans (the 'Kittim') came to Palestine. The historian Josephus (AD 37–?100) named some

individual Essenes as prophets, but they seem rather to have been diviners. The Essenes, like Jesus, denounced the wickedness and the failings of the Jewish priestly class, the leaders of the people, but this is a characteristic of so much Jewish prophecy that it does not offer a real comparison. Jesus' prophecy of the catastrophic end of world order, as reported in Mark 13, makes an overt reference to the earlier prediction of such terrible events in the Book of Daniel.

The execution of Jesus did not have the effect of silencing his closest followers. It probably was not thought necessary to silence them, because none was arrested at the time. Understandably, their immediate reaction to the execution was one of bewilderment and defeat. But the strange discovery of his empty tomb, and their experiences of some sort of encounter with Jesus after his death, caused the faithful disciples, relatives and followers to cohere into a group that preserved belief in Jesus' messianic mission. Its centre was in Jerusalem, not in Galilee, from where the key figures in the movement came, and where some of them had initially returned after his death. Its focus seems to have been his disciple, Peter, and Jesus' own family. Among the family, the most important was James (Jacob), a brother of Jesus, who a generation later was tried and executed by the then Jewish high priest, Ananus. Before his death, James and Peter had had dealings with Paul of Tarsus that show the Jesus-followers in Jerusalem to have been conforming Jews, as Jesus had been.

But when ye shall see the abomination of desolation spoken of by Daniel the prophet, standing where it ought not (let him that readeth understand) then let them that be in Judaea flee to the mountains. (Mark 13:14)

Below: A stone slab from a sepulchre in Rome showing the apostles Peter and Paul. After the death of Jesus, his disciple Peter, members of his family, and later Paul of Tarsus, continued to carry and preach his message.

The Jerusalem group was critical for the transmission of the memory of Jesus' person and the content of his message. Without it, these would have become even less known to posterity than the doctrines of the Essenes. Its audience, to which the good news about Jesus the anointed one of God (the Messiah) was preached, remained essentially Jewish. Jesus was not, after all, the last Messiah to be proclaimed among the Jews: there are examples from sixteenth-century Palestine, and from times much closer to our own.

St Paul and the Spreading of the Word

Where Gentiles were won over to accept Messiah-Jesus, as started to happen in Antioch as well as in Jerusalem, the males had to accept circumcision, and all the converts were subjected to Jewish dietary laws. It was not inconceivable that such a Jewish sub-cult might arrive, eventually, at a strong position within the Judaism of the Roman Empire. The Jews outside Palestine numbered several millions, and Jewish proselytism was far from new.

Because it was known that Jesus had not refused contact with Gentiles, and had even performed healings in their households, the question was bound to arise: might his message be preached differently to Gentiles and Jews? The question was eventually put, by Paul of Tarsus, in a manner that revealed extraordinary spiritual and moral gifts, besides a ruthless power of character. Paul's life as a follower of Jesus placed a clear boundary between the group of disciples and relatives who had experienced an encounter with Jesus after his death, and the 'churches' that subsequently became the main bearers of his message.

Paul was an articulate and educated Jew from a prosperous and populous city in the south-west of Asia Minor, whose family had obtained the envied privilege of Roman citizenship. He was literate in both Hebrew and Greek (although not necessarily highly competent in the latter), and passionately committed to the Jewish religion. His recent biographer, Jerome Murphy-O'Connor, thinks his birth year was not too distant from that of Jesus, shortly before the beginning of the Common Era. Paul's parents may have been Pharisees, an observant Jewish sect that had, in the past, played some political role but that in Paul's time was mostly a table-fellowship whose members had some influence in religious circles. Paul himself joined the sect, probably while living in Jerusalem, and later considered himself to have been, as a young man, learned in Jewish law. He was initially a vigorous enemy of the followers of Jesus.

It is argued that the apostle Luke overstated the legal authority Paul could have enjoyed as a Pharisee, even if he had belonged to the Jewish supreme religious court, to seek out the Jesus sect, and order their punishment [Acts: 22:4-5; 26:12]. There are particular doubts about the draconian legal powers attributed to him in Damascus, a Roman province far from Judaea, where it is unlikely that Jewish religious authorities in Jerusalem would have enjoyed any legal powers at all. At the least, Paul denounced the followers of Jesus ruthlessly whenever he could smell them out, and was loud in his condemnations. How long he behaved in this manner is unknown, it might have been for months, or years.

Paul refers to the circumstances of his conversion outside Damascus in a very elliptical way, in a context [I Cor.15] that prefaces his testimony by a short creed which asserts the resurrection of Jesus after his death, 'according to the scriptures'. Paul then relates his own version of the 'appearances' of Jesus after death, first to Peter and to the twelve disciples, then to 'over five hundred of our brothers

---

And I persecuted this way unto the death, binding and delivering into prisons both men and women.

As also the high priest doth bear me witness and all the estate of the elders: from whom also I received letters unto the brethren, and went to Damascus, to bring them which were there bound unto Jerusalem for to be punished. (Acts 22: 4-5)

at once, most of whom are still alive', then to James and the apostles, and finally to Paul himself. Paul's recognition of the manifestation of this risen Jesus to himself comes in a sense to finish the story, at the end of a series of earlier appearances of Jesus to others. And indeed, it should have been near the end of the story, given the belief by Paul's generation of Jesus-followers in a proximate coming of God's kingdom. From Paul's recognition of the risen Jesus came the power of his call to faith and apostolate, which endured through a long and often harsh life, until his martyrdom in Rome.

Paul later attributed the manifestation of Jesus that he had experienced outside Damascus to a divine order that he should proclaim Jesus among the Gentiles. But this mission took years to assume a definite shape. It was three years before he fled Damascus – after an abortive and probably brief journey in the Nabataean kingdom south of Damascus – and visited Peter and the Jesus-fellowship in Jerusalem. In one way, the Jesus apparition was enough for Paul, but conventional information about Jesus must have been short. There may already have been writings, but perhaps not. If there was insufficient or no written tradition about his life, the surviving relatives and disciples had to be asked.

If the account in Acts (10) is correct – and some have thought it to be a fictitious interpolation made to justify the missionary opening to the Gentiles – the critical moment for the Jerusalem community must have followed Peter's conversion of the Roman officer, Cornelius, in the garrison town of Caesarea. This is said to have followed Peter's vision of a heavenly visitation that told him to cease making the distinctions, incumbent on any practising Jew, between 'clean' and 'unclean' objects (and, by implication, people). Peter is said to have baptized not only Cornelius himself, but also all those other Gentiles standing by who were equally accepting of Peter's message, and who were thought to have 'received the Holy Spirit' (and, according to Acts, the gift of ecstatic utterance) equally with Cornelius. On his return to Jerusalem, Peter is said to have convinced the Jewish Jesus-fellowship of the validity of the acceptance of Gentiles for baptism.

Paul had returned to his own area of Cilicia in Asia Minor, and to Antioch on the River Orontes, and preached the Gospel there alongside a Jesus-follower called Barnabas. He then carried his message to an area that must have presented him with a new kind of challenge: the predominantly rural, military and Celtic society of Galatia, in the central plateau of Asia Minor. Why he should have gone to this isolated area is a bit of a puzzle; he may have formed a resolution to take his mission there while he was preaching in Pisidian Antioch.

Eight years later, Paul's apostolate took him across the Bosphorus into Europe and Macedonia. There he spent two years in the cities of Thessalonica and Phillipi with predominantly Gentile converts, strengthening them in what may now be called the new religion. From there he went on to Athens and Corinth. How lacking in sharp definition this new religion still was, outside a few convictions about Jesus, and about the approaching end of all things, emerges from Paul's letters. His mission to these communities was not to legislate, but to

Below: The altar in St Peter's Church in Antioch, southern Turkey. Following his conversion to Christianity, Paul preached at Antioch and set off on his missionary journey from here.

© Sonia Halliday Photographs

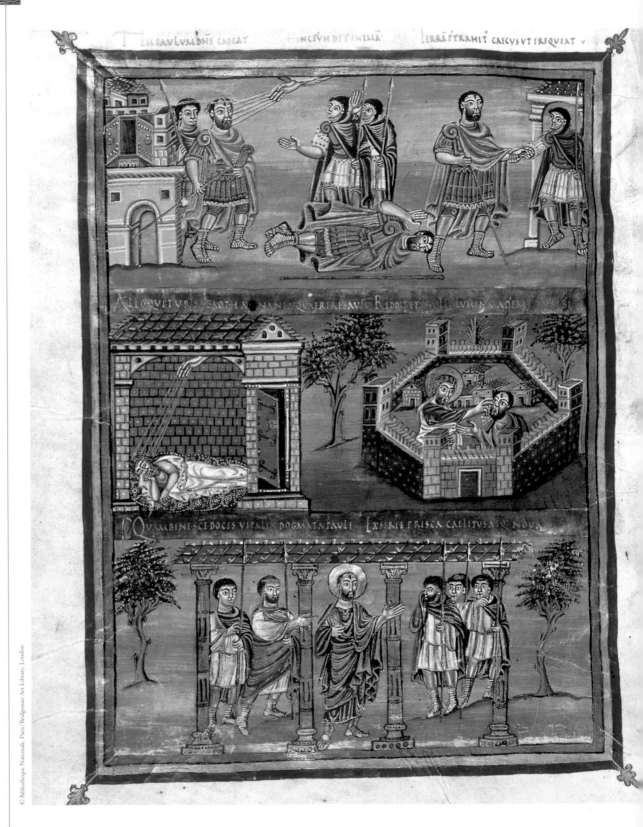

Right: The conversion of Paul and scenes of Paul preaching. The illustration comes from a ninth-century Bible made for Charles I of France, also known as Charles the Bald, emperor of the West (875–77).

strengthen their sense of identity and common moral purpose, and to 'pass on the tradition of the way we must live to please God.' The designation of 'Christians', from the messianic title of Jesus as Christos, the anointed one, was only one of several used to describe them.

In Athens and in Corinth Paul was in the geographical historic centre of Greek culture. In Luke's account of Paul at bay among the Athenian intellectuals in the Areopagus [Acts 17], there is a sharp sense of the historic clash between Jewish fideism and Greek scepticism that took place. It was a dispute that Paul clearly lost, because some of those present mocked him, and others prevaricated. Some were convinced, but there is no mention of an Athenian church. In Corinth he had better fortune, although the traditionally pleasure-loving society proved quite resistant to the severe way of life that Paul seems to have to some extent taken for granted among his converts.

In Galatia, Paul may have gone outside the towns, which would have been more modest and isolated than those in Cilicia, Palestine and Syria. The main thrust of Paul's missionary effort was not rustic; it was located where it might have been expected to take place in an ancient world entirely dominated by the power and privilege of the city. The theatres for his propagandist effort were the public places offered by the ancient city: the public square, the synagogue and the lecture hall. The house-churches – which were just rooms in dwelling houses – were the natural meeting places where the followers of the religion could meet, eat a communal meal, speak of their faith, and acquire a sense of communal identity. However, while potential converts could be introduced there singly, there could be no general outreach in the house-church to a pagan or a Jewish public.

The natural tendency for Paul was to speak in the Jewish synagogue, as Jesus had done. To Jesus-believing Jews it must have seemed that the synagogue was itself the natural meeting place, to be used by all when the process of convincing Jewry of the righteous cause of Jesus had been terminated – or abandoned when the proximate end of time and the proclamation of God's kingdom came. Neither expectation was fulfilled. The first Christian churches to be substantial public buildings were not to be built for another two centuries.

Paul, Peter and the Conversion of Gentiles

The question of leadership and direction in the new cult came up decisively in AD 51, when Paul and Barnabas visited Jerusalem, probably with a mandate from the Christians in Antioch, to decide whether Christian male converts ought to be circumcised and, by implication, submitted to the full requirements of Jewish traditional law and dietary custom. The problem did not only affect Antioch. It was common to all the missions in Europe and Asia Minor. At a meeting with the Jerusalem leaders, Paul claimed the issues of policy and status were decided in his favour. James, Peter and John accepted his claims (and those of Barnabas) to leadership of the mission to the Gentiles, and agreed not to press the issue of circumcision of Gentile converts. This was not only a theological issue, but also a practical one. Christianity became vastly more accessible the moment that its male converts no longer had to submit to a worrying and painful surgical operation from which they might take quite a long time to recover. At the same time that Paul made this momentous agreement, he agreed to forward charitable contributions from the diaspora Christians for the community in Jerusalem.

The matter was too delicate to be amicably settled at a stroke. Possibly after the Jerusalem agreement it reappeared in the form of a dispute over dietary laws between Paul and Peter, when the latter was in Antioch. Peter, influenced by pressure from James in Jerusalem and supported, to Paul's

Therefore disputed he in the synagogue with the Jews, and with the devout persons, and in the market daily with them that met with him.
Then certain philosophers of the Epicureans, and some of the Stoicks, encountered him. And some said, What will this babbler say? other some, He seemeth to be a setter forth of strange gods: because he preached unto them Jesus, and the resurrection.
And they took him, and brought him unto Areopagus, saying, May we know what this new doctrine whereof thou speakest, is?
(Acts: 17: 17, 18, 19)

Above: Carved relief from a marble Christian sarcophagus dating from the end of the fourth century. It shows Christ with his apostles.

indignation, by Barnabas, refused to share meals with the Gentile Christians in Antioch. It may sound a magnification of trivia to modern Western ears, but it was not. Hospitality was a solemn matter in the ancient world and conferred a form of kinship, as it still does in the Middle East. So a refusal to participate in a non-kosher meal was not just peevish, but a denial of belonging to the same society. To an ex-Pharisee such as Paul, who had lived in a community where two-thirds of the special rules known to us concern diet, Peter's refusal to eat the common meal was extremely serious. Four or five years later, when he was again in Corinth, Paul was still conscious of the estrangement with Peter. At this point it is possible to speak of the churches of Asia and Europe. The Greek term for a church means those who are called to the assembly. The quarrel between Judaizers, who thought the Levitical laws in the Old Testament were still binding for Christians, and those who sided against them with Paul, continued. This was especially true in Galatia, where perhaps the strength of Greek culture with its assertion of natural law and morality was weaker than elsewhere and where, consequently, the novice Christians felt the need for the more comprehensive support of Judaism. Paul tended to assume the moral framework of Judaism without spelling it out. His dramatic assertion of the claims of the spirit over the law has tended to puzzle the more timid souls, up to our own time.

© Louvre, Paris, France/Bridgeman Art Library, London

When Paul resumed his missionary journeys, he continued to target the great centres of population that he judged to be accessible to his efforts. A great prize was Ephesus, one of the great economic and cultural centres of Asia Minor, with a population of at least 150,000, and an ampitheatre judged by contemporaries to be one of the wonders of the world. It may be that his efforts in Ephesus cost Paul a period of imprisonment.

The hostility of the orthodox Jews of Jerusalem led to the troubled final period of Paul's life, during which he was moved about the Mediterranean at the behest of Roman justice. He had perhaps come to Jerusalem to bring the contributions from the Christians in the churches that he supervised, to the church in Jerusalem. After his arrival he was accused by the Asian Jews in Jerusalem of smuggling a Gentile into the forbidden sacred areas of the Temple, and they tried to lynch him. Roman troops intervened, and sent him under protective custody to their headquarters in Caesarea. Paul claimed Roman citizenship, but was still held in custody in Caesarea for two years or longer. Finally, a new governor sent him to Rome for trial. And in Rome, after a further unknown period of custody – perhaps for a time, only of house arrest – he was put to death during the anti-Christian measures of Emperor Nero, no later than AD 68. Peter was executed in Rome during the same period and for the same reason, although the history of Peter's presence in Rome is unknown.

© Ronald Sheridan, Ancient Art & Architecture Collection

Above: The great amphitheatre at Ephesus, which dates back to the first century AD. During Paul's time Ephesus was a wealthy cultural and economic centre. Paul visited the city and addressed an epistle to the Christians.

23

Some seventy years after the death of Jesus, the churches Peter and Paul had established, and those set up by other followers, were scattered over a vast area of the eastern Roman Empire and a good part of the western, including Rome itself. The numbers of Christians were still very modest, but their communities were so tenaciously and bravely supported that they became a new factor in the cultural and religious life of the Empire. The Christian congregations saw their obedience to Jesus as a prelude to the coming of God's kingdom, and not as some new chapter in the history of human power. Yet Christianity was still only a minor, novel cult. Power was to remain, for at least another century, something that Christians recognized in human relationships, but repudiated for themselves. However, the churches were already near a point where, if we look at them as part of human history and not as part of salvation history, power was to drift towards them whether they wanted it or not.

Right: The Roman Emperor Nero (AD 37–68). A virulent anti-Christian, Nero introduced a wave of persecutions during which both Paul and Peter were put to death.

Left: A first-century terracotta statuette of a Christian priest. Within seventy years of Jesus' death, Christians still only numbered a few but their early churches and communities were established.

2

PERSECUTORS AND MARTYRS

It is hard to conceive of Christianity without the Roman Empire. No one who has written about it, from the authors of the Gospel of Luke onwards, has failed to make the connection, even if only in the negative context of persecution. Luke made a incorrect statement about a supposed census decree of the Emperor Augustus (63 BC–AD 14), which he made responsible for a fictional journey of Mary and Joseph to Bethlehem, so that the birth of the Messiah could be said to have taken place in the exact locality that the Jewish scriptures required. There was no such decree, and the Roman legate Quirinius, mentioned by Luke as being in office at the time, did not arrive in Syria until nine or ten years after the probable birth date of Jesus. These things are not important for the credibility of the historical Jesus. But they are important, in that the authors of one of the pillar texts of the religion chose to anchor the incarnate appearance of its founder in time by attaching two great figures of Roman power, the Emperor and the Legate.

Without the great grid of the Roman Empire, which established a common regime and ruling culture from the Parthian to the British and Moroccan frontiers, the followers of Jesus could never have taken the message of salvation to earth's farthest bounds, as first-century Hellenized Jews conceived those bounds. Nor could the ideas of the celestial and terrestrial cities of God have come into being. These inspired St Augustine, four centuries after Christ, to conceive a Christianity that, as it were, stood on the shoulders of the transformed Empire. To Augustine, God had given the Romans the arts and practice of dominion, and the imposition of a kind of peace, although the Romans had failed even to give effect to the ideals of justice that they served.

Was Christianity really a subversive force that proved hostile to the Roman Empire? A thousand years after the birth of Christ, a Roman Emperor still ruled a great Empire in the East, led great Roman armies, and ruled over a version of the Roman senatorial aristocracy. In the West at the same time a barbarian ruler sought recognition as a Roman Emperor, and presided over a version of the

Left: The synagogue at Dura-Europos, Syria.

Above: The apotheosis of Caesar in AD 161. In pre-Christianized Rome, the Emperor was welcomed into the pantheon of existing gods and worshipped as a living deity. This marble slab shows Marcus Aurelius, who ruled from AD 161–180, who renewed the persecutions of Christians.

Imperial Roman court. Today, two thousand years after the birth of Christ, a Christian bishop of Rome, wearing a costume reminiscent of that once worn by Roman Senators, flies all over the world to his flock. He speaks, when necessary, an inflected dialect of Latin, and the doctrines he preaches (many of which have been codified in the Latin tongue) are full of echoes of the supremely Roman principles of order and decorum, and of historical survivals of the religion's remote late-Roman past.

The Roman Empire was one of the greatest autocracies the world has known, supported by a large civil service, a huge army and a powerful secret police. It was perhaps not efficient in the modern sense, but terrifyingly effective when it felt it had really identified an enemy. Over the at-first obscure Jewish cult of Christianity, it hesitated for a very long time between bad-tempered proscription and

Left: Bacchanalian abandon on a sarcophagus fragment; Roman authority treated early Christianity with the same suspicion it had directed towards the pagan cult of Bacchus in the second century BC.

contemptuous quasi-toleration. It was made aware of the cult's existence at quite an early stage, because of the converts it had made in the capital, even in or near the Imperial Court.

Christianity was sometimes felt by the Roman ruling class to be subversive because, even more than that of its Jewish parent, its monotheism, or doctrine of one single god, cut at the basic social cohesive force of Roman religion, that was not so much a state religion as a religion of the state. In Japan there is a modern parallel in Shintoism, which makes certain shrines into imperial and national shrines. The many gods that were worshipped in the Empire were not incompatible with the official religion, which could also take the form of worship of the personal divinity of the Emperor.

However, in the past certain foreign pagan gods had awakened deep political disquiet in Rome. The accusation of 'depraved religion' had once been made against the new cult of the Greek god, Dionysus, known to the Romans as Bacchus, who was worshipped in secret, supposedly orgiastic rites. Fear of a Bacchanal secret society resembled later Roman suspicion of the Christians. The nearest modern equivalent is suspicion of the Freemasons. In 186 BC the Bacchanal scandal became a major political panic about possible treason in Rome, and led to the execution of a good many of its adepts.

Christians refused to make the libation of incense and wine before the Emperor's statue and the images of the gods, so demonstrating – though only on the occasions when specifically asked to conform – their impiety and disloyalty. As well as these acts of open dissidence, Christians were also sometimes noted to display a sort of obstinate and disparaging attitude towards the traditional religions, which did not make them friends.

Left: Trajan's Column, Rome, built in AD113. The Emperor Trajan left a permanent record of his achievements in the shape of a column with graphic depictions of his military and civil triumphs. His policy towards Christianity was a pragmatic one, designed to diffuse anti-Christian hysteria and civil unrest.

Above: A gold coin, or aureus, minted in the reign of the Emperor Hadrian (AD117–138). While not actively encouraging Christianity, he did not oppose it, reserving his intolerance for the Jews who were rebelling against Roman rule.

31

© Yale University Art Gallery, Dura Europos Archive

Right: The baptistry of a Christian house-church at Dura-Europos. Its simplicity was a marked contrast to the lavish and highly decorated synagogue in the same town.

Like many governing classes, that of the Roman Empire was prone to bouts of xenophobic suspicion. The Jews, with their single, exclusive god, their practice of circumcision and their recent participation in the Palestinian rebellions, were an obvious target. So too was their Christian offshoot, whose abandonment of circumcision could be seen as having rendered them even more socially dangerous. In the last decade of the first century the Emperor Domitian seems to have suffered an attack of acute insecurity. Not only did he proclaim his own divinity and require worship, but he also had members of his own family executed on the suspicion of 'atheism' and consorting with foreign religions. This atmosphere was dangerous to both Christians and Jews, especially in the east of the Empire where both groups were unpopular. Later, in the first half of the second century, the eastern Jews took part in two further major revolts. The repressions that followed were severe.

As the end of the first century of the Common Era approached, the tie with Judaism that had been vitally important in the first years after the death of Jesus, became subject first to a slow and then to a brusque estrangement, although a form of Judaic Christian church persisted in Palestine for a long period. The estrangement was mutual: formal denunciations of the Christians were pronounced in some synagogues. Quite separately from their mutual disagreements, and for different reasons, both Christians and Jews incurred government distrust and displeasure. St Ignatius of Antioch, who was martyred in the early years of the second century, wrote: 'It is absurd to talk of Jesus Christ and to practise Judaism. After all, Judaism believed in Christianity, not Christianity in Judaism'.

Perhaps a possible modern comparison would be the paranoid fear of Communism widespread in the United States from the late 1930s onwards, which produced the Congressional Un-American Activities Committee of 1938, and lay behind the McCarthyite persecutions of the 1950s. Once an issue is defined as the defence of a way of life, the advocates of a conspiracy theory have scope to demand arbitrary action against the hidden enemy. On the other hand, other establishment elites may be more confident about the resilience of official culture, and may resist the tendency to panic.

Trajan and the Beginnings of Toleration

In Imperial Rome very few people were prepared to say that members of a religion, which refused formal allegiance to the state gods, and who met in secret, were worthy of anything but severe punishment. But there were powerful people, sometimes including the Emperor himself, who were not disposed to make the refusal of some religious fanatics to conform to the letter of the observance of state ceremonies into a big issue. That seems to have been the upshot of the discussions between Pliny the Younger (AD 62–?114), the provincial governor of Pontus-Bithynia in Asia Minor, and the Emperor Trajan (AD 53–117), when the former asked the Emperor for guidance on how to treat Christians who were denounced for disloyalty.

The Emperor decided how denunciations were to be treated in future. Instead of encouraging people to inform against the Christians, he discouraged them by invoking the normal procedure in calumny cases. If charges could not be substantiated, the whole weight of the criminal penalty was visited on the accuser. Trajan also gave accused Christians the chance to renounce the religion, and so free themselves, after accusation. This was not toleration, but it was a policy of live and let live that discouraged anti-Christian fever, and gave Christianity many chances to continue to preach its mission. A decade later the Emperor Hadrian (AD 76–138) was to maintain a similar policy towards the Christians.

Above: A Christian martyred at the stake, as shown in a Byzantine manuscript. After a century or so of toleration, Christianity became a political target for the Emperor Marcus Aurelius and many of the faithful were martyred for their faith.

Left: The synagogue at Dura-Europos in Syria, an area sufficiently remote from the Emperor Hadrian's anti-Jewish policy. While the city of Jerusalem had lost even its name, large and richly decorated synagogues were built in and around the Near East. The frescoes show scenes from the Old Testament.

33

Right: A marble slab showing a public sacrificial procession with animals to be immolated for Mars. Roman people were suspicious of the privacy of Christian meetings. Christians refused to take part in the pagan rituals which would publicly show allegiance to the Roman gods and thus the Roman state.

© AKG London / Erich Lessing

Hadrian's policy towards the Jews, who had supported armed rebellions, and were to mount a further, final rebellion in AD 132–5, was far less favourable. Hadrian abolished even the name of Jerusalem: he renamed the city Aelia Capitolina, and by AD 310 the old name was so far forgotten that a Roman governor of the nearby city of Caesarea had no idea that a city called Jerusalem had ever existed. But this did not mean that Judaism was finished as a proselytizing force in the Graeco-Roman world, nor that it could not prosper. Synagogues continued to be built all over the Near East; in Dura-Europos, on the Euphrates, the synagogue expanded in size, wealth and decoration in a much more impressive way than the little house-church of the Christians in the same frontier town. While Christians still succeeded in converting Jews, Jews still quite often succeeded in converting Christians.

Persecution of Christians by the Roman authorities began with Nero's repression of AD 64. It was only sporadic after that until the great persecutions of AD 165–180, which included the terrible severities inflicted upon Christians of Lyons in AD 177. The temper of martyrdom was forged during that period.

The Secret of Christian Rituals

At the same time that Christianity finally fell away from Judaism, great cultural gaps between pagan and Christian began to appear. For a long period, the main problem that Christians faced was that of ignorance about their religion on the part of the pagans. The privacy of their meetings, and the known big variations in class and status of their members, meant that they were vulnerable to suspicion of unspeakable crime: of infant sacrifice, of incest, of cannibalism.

Right: The slab marking St Paul's tomb in the church of St Paul's Outside the Walls, Rome. It is marked with the letters PAULO APOSTOLO MART. Balsam was poured through the holes on to the saint's body. The faithful used to lower pieces of cloth to soak up the balsam, to be kept as holy relics.

Taken from *The Tombs of St Peter and St Paul*, E Kirschbaum S J, 1959.

The innocent truth about Christian meetings for worship, which at this point could only take place in rooms in Christian houses, and the equal innocence of their religious common meals, began after a long time to come to light. Even while Christians gradually ceased to be suspected of the most nefarious crimes, their other big differences from majority culture were noticed. For example, the reverence and familiar worship that Christians accorded to their martyred dead shocked the pagan world. It broke the taboo that in traditional culture an unbridgeable gulf separated the dead from the living. When Virgil's hero, Aeneas, descended to the underworld, he could speak to the pale spirits of the dead only across the blood of the sacrifices he had made. To the Christians, their dead only slept, to awake in the Lord on the Last Day.

By the third century the communion of the living Christians with their dead martyrs was achieved not only in the eucharistic feast, but also from the physical contact that they insisted on making with the tombs. In the slab that marks the tomb of St Paul, there are holes through which the faithful poured balsam. The openings served to let down small cloths. Once they had soaked up the perfumes poured into the tomb, they were recovered and regarded as precious relics. Allied to this (although more compatible with pagan custom) was the practice of a kind of funerary feasting at the tombs of the saints, a usage that St Augustine half excused, but, in the end, condemned, in his own mother.

The Concept of Charity

Christianity spread through the Mediterranean, including North Africa and Spain, and to the Near East. By the second half of the second century, it had spread to the Rhone valley. To what extent or in what areas the settled Jewish communities acted as springboards for this expansion is uncertain. It may be that Greek-speakers were the key transmitters. The expansion was probably still very modest. Socially it was notoriously a religion that took converts from every class of ancient society, from slaves to a sprinkling of members of big land-owning and merchant families. Artisans and freedmen supplied a good number of Christians, but firm evidence for numbers and proportions is scarce.

It is unlikely that slaves were disproportionately numerous in the Christian communities. There was no internal pressure on slave-owning Christians to free their slaves, and church leaders told slaves to obey their masters. It is even possible that manumissions of slaves by Christian slave-owners were less frequent than among pagans, because married male Christians were forbidden the sexual contact with female slaves that was normal to a pagan slave-owner. Such contact was one of the main stimuli to grant freedom to the slave mother and child. However, church funds were sometimes used to buy the freedom of Christian slaves of pagan masters.

One function of the churches was to act as friendly societies, whose charity looked after their members irrespective of social class. 'See, how these Christians love each other' was a frequent pagan comment. Not only the indigent, who among other things were helped with the decorous burial of their dead, but also members of classes above this were assisted. Help was given in particular to widows, whose remarriage was discouraged, and unmarried young women, who perhaps were unmarried because of their lack of a dowry, but who were helped to maintain their celibate state. Foundlings were often cared for by the churches. Sickness or imprisonment, above all imprisonment for religion, also attracted community assistance.

The churches could not have their own finances because Roman law did not recognize them as bodies capable of owning property. But the body of clergy that had grown up to supply leadership

Right: Mural painting from the sixth century in the catacombs of San Callisto, Rome. The saints Calixtus and Cyprian are shown together. St Calixtus, released from prison after the intercession of Marcia, a concubine of the Emperor Commodus, became pope in AD 218 but was martyred four years later. St Cyprian (c.AD 200–258), became Bishop of Carthage in AD 248, but was martyred a decade later during the reign of the Emperor Valerian.

and to look after liturgical and practical needs was recognized to have a material claim on the local believers. From an early point the clergy, or at least its main members, were not expected to follow their own secular callings. In the larger churches an organized clergy included deacons in charge of social services, readers, acolytes, exorcists, doorkeepers.

Women and Celibacy

Women, although without clerical status, were extremely important in the Christian community. The prophetess was not unknown, nor without honour. Some Christian women were rich ladies, although not, during the first two centuries, from senatorial families. If women of such rank wanted unions with Christian men, they had to have them outside marriage, as there were no marriageable Christian men of their own class. Women could exercise political influence on behalf of the Church from unexpected places. Marcia, the concubine of the Emperor Commodus (AD180–92), was instrumental in securing the release of Christian prisoners from the mines. One of the released detainees was a certain Calixtus, later Bishop of Rome, who was the first of several popes to have been closely connected with the banking industry, although the later examples occurred only after a gap of many centuries.

Both men and women in the Christian congregations were affected by the emphasis on celibacy, which severely discouraged remarriage for either sex. Women were especially affected, too, by the social provision of funds to help them survive a long widowhood. Persuading young women to value an indefinite chastity had a very strong social effect. This had not always been so: at the beginning the lack of discrimination between the sexes in the Christian groups had been one of the things that caused most scandal among pagans. The growing emphasis on chastity as a virtue may have owed something to St Paul, but more to the wish of the priests to be distinguished from the other males in the community. Not that the married state was entirely forgotten: at the end of the second century St Clement of Alexandria devoted a lot of sympathetic attention to the moral problems of married Christians.

Part of the coherence and resilience of the Christian communities was due to the rigorous and often long apprenticeship imposed upon converts. The status of a catechumen, or Christian receiving instruction, meant that for a period of years – or, in the case of catechumens who deferred baptism until the last possible moment before death, for most of their lives – converts accepted a life in which they were in an important sense still outside the main body of believers. Together with the penitents who were deemed to have fallen from grace, they were offered bread that was not the bread given at the sacred communal meal, and restricted in how they participated in the communal life of the group. It was a subclass of believers still maintained, at least until times within living memory, in Ethiopia. In the ancient world, similar distinctions between the novices and the adepts would have been familiar to followers of other contemporary religions.

The Rite of Baptism

Baptism, in the Christian regime, was the rite that marked the passage of a man or a woman (or a child, for they also were provided for) from the profane to the sacred life.[1] The detailed prescriptions for the ceremony, dating from the early third century, are starkly explicit. Baptism was to take place at dawn on a Sunday, after an all-night vigil and administered, if possible, in running water. Witnesses were interrogated about the suitability of the candidates. According to the Roman priest Hippolytus,

Below: Roman mural painting of first to third century. Women played an important role in the spread and maintenance of Christianity. Many were martyred.

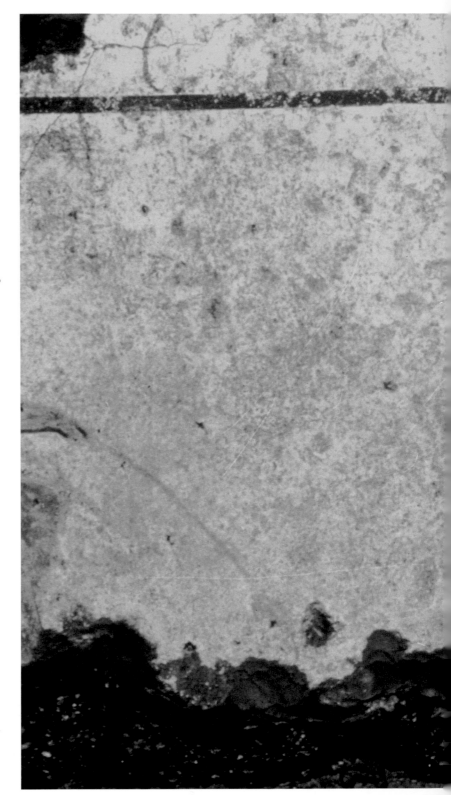

who wrote the tract, people from quite a long list of callings and moral categories were to be excluded from baptism. The list includes pimps, prostitutes, actors, homosexuals, gladiators, magicians and army officers who give orders to kill — the history of Christianity would have been very different if the last prohibition had been maintained. In the days leading up to baptism the candidate was given repeated exorcisms to reveal and excise impurity, and then, after a devotional night and a final exorcism-anointment, was led naked to the water: the women, at this point, took off their jewellery. There was a final interrogation about past moral conduct, and about the reasons for asking for baptism.

Then the liturgy took its course: the candidate renounced the Devil and his works, and pronounced the Creed, as the bishop gave the neophyte a triple immersion in the waters. No one who had experienced these sacramental solemnities, and the long apprenticeship leading up to them, was going to take the Christian commitment lightly.

1 P. Cramer, *Baptism and Change in the Early Middle Ages*, c.200–c.1150 (Cambridge,1993), pp.9–45

Left: Fresco from the catacombs of San Callisto, Rome. A baptism scene from the third century emphasizes how significant the ritual was in the new faith. Baptism was prefaced by long and elaborate preparation and was not lightly undertaken.

3

CHRISTIANS IN A PAGAN WORLD

Christian persecution resumed in the second half of the second century. The bishops were the leaders of the Christian communities and they did not refuse to bear witness. In Smyrna (Izmir) in Asia Minor, the bishop was the 86-year-old Polycarp, a leader well known as far as Rome and Lyons. He was also remembered as the one-time host of Ignatius, the Bishop of Antioch who was then being escorted to Rome for martyrdom, and he had known St John the Divine. Polycarp was known to and respected by the civic authorities in Smyrna, who nevertheless had to bring him before the Roman provincial governor. The proconsul was willing to allow him to address the pagan and Jewish mob in the stadium where he had been taken after his arrest, but Polycarp declined, perhaps knowing that it would only inflame passions further; he expressed himself willing to discuss his religion further with the governor, but not with the people. He could not be thrown to the beasts, as the governor had closed the so-called Games, but was forthwith burned in the stadium. Significantly, after his death, his remains were retained, to stop Christians from using them as sacred relics.

Hostility to Christians was not just the work of people who wanted more human bloodshed in the circus: it had a rational, conservative basis. By this point, the anti-Christian movement essentially rested on the widespread popular feeling that some corrupting internal force was at work to undermine traditional cultural values. That these were the feelings of 'the mob' does not mean that they were of the people and therefore to be disparaged: historians have analysed 'the mob' in the context of modern history, and found that it often included large numbers of very 'respectable' citizens.

One who put up a rational argument against the Christians was an intellectual called Celsus who wrote a polemic work against the Christians. His arguments have not survived in a complete form, but they were in general those of an enlightened stoic who saw the Roman Empire as the protector and defender of local gods and civic custom, and the guarantor of peace and justice. The Jews and the Christians, but particularly the latter, were the advocates of a pernicious and dangerous religious

Left: Detail showing Jonah and the whale from a fourth-century mosaic.

Right: A stone frieze showing a Roman butcher at work. Christianity welcomed people of all classes on an equal basis. For anti-Christians, such as Celsus, this represented a threat to traditional values.

Below: A bust of the Emperor Decius (c.AD 200–251). Under his rule, Christians were persecuted with great severity.

particularism, who both peddled versions of a divinely chosen people whose destiny excluded everyone else. The Christians, who had 'spread to become a multitude', were also dangerous because they threatened to impose the values of the ignorant upon the rest of the community.

> '*In private houses we see woolworkers, cobblers, laundry men, and the most illiterate and bucolic yokels, who would not dare say anything at all in front of their elders and their more intelligent masters. But whenever they get hold of children in private and some stupid women with them, they let out some astounding statements... They alone, they say, know the right way to live...*'

However, Celsus mocked Christian Messianism on account of its practical impotence. In the crises of the prosecution of Christian impiety, their God had singularly failed to intervene on behalf of any of them.

The heroism of Christians must be saluted. Their movement remains to this day the most important passive and peaceful resistance to an autocratic government to have occurred anywhere in the western world. Not that the Christians rejected all Roman government; they protested their loyalty, and their refusal concerned only the submission they were told to make to demonic idols. Nor did they all with one accord choose martyrdom: on the contrary, in the persecution (AD 249–51), of the Emperor Decius, the apostasy of an overwhelming majority in a Christian congregation was not infrequent. But the strength and constancy of many Christian witnesses remained in the face of terrible punishments. A moving and probably genuine prison diary has survived from the persecutions of Carthage at the beginning of the third century, by a lady called Perpetua, who was martyred together with her slave, but who, while awaiting martyrdom, recorded her dreams and spiritual experiences.

Apostasy and Martyrdom

The heroism of the few inevitably meant judgement on the poltroonery of the many. There have always been those whose conviction in moments of great trial proves inferior to that of the strongest. Muhammad's attitude to such people, 'waverers' or 'hypocrites', was severe. The Christian attitude was less severe, but it did not exclude rigorism. If the lapsed Christians wanted to return to the communities of the faithful when the danger had passed, the attitude of the surviving confessors was not necessarily vindictive. But there was among them a very strong doubt that, after such a decisive apostasy, there was any authority in the Christian community to forgive such things. Or, if there was, many of them thought that the returned apostate could be absolved only when at the point of death.

The issue about the absolution of returned apostates was critical to the future of Christianity. If the penitent apostate could not be reintegrated into the community of the people of God, the Christian groups were destined to become a narrowed sect. The matter came to a head in Rome, where the rigorist position was led by a Roman priest called Novation (*fl.* third century), who eventually felt it his duty to seek election as Bishop of Rome, and in Carthage, where a severe but still not absolutely inflexible position was assumed by Bishop Cyprian (c.AD200–258). Novation was opposed in Rome by a party of leniency, whose candidate, the deacon Cornelius, got a majority vote. Cyprian hesitated over which candidate he should support for the Roman bishopric, because the issue so closely concerned his own church. Eventually he opted for Cornelius and so, implicitly, for a policy of mercy.

Tied up with the matter of receiving apostates back into the fold was the the question of the authority of bishops. If dealing with returned apostates was going to be left to the congregation, and so to the surviving confessors, rather than to the bishop, they were going to be harshly done by. If the bishop had the power of absolution, the community of Christians was going to be ready to compromise, and to pardon the lapsed believer. The debate in the end concerned the place of ordinary mortals in the Church.

Another hidden danger of the big persecutions was that Christians would come to see martyrdom as an end in itself. 'Do not look forward to dying in your bed, in childbirth or

Below: A mosaic pavement illustrates Jonah being spat out by the whale. Early Christians used the Old Testament story of Jonah being swallowed and spat out as an allegory for the Resurrection.

© Basilica, Aquileia, Italy/Bridgeman Art Library, London

in the lassitude of fever, but in martyrdom so that he who has suffered for you may be glorified.' This doctrine of the Montanists, an extremist Christian wing that originated in Phrygia, in Asia Minor, is not entirely unfamiliar to our own generation, although in an Islamic, not Christian context, and in a warlike rather than a passive form.

Apologists for Christ

There was persecution of Christians not only in Asia, but at the other end of the Empire, at Lyons in the Rhone valley. But towards the end of the second century the persecutions died down again. The Roman Empire was experiencing a time of reduced internal and external tensions, and the big wars on the borders, though never entirely quietened, were for a time less exacting. The cities of the provinces reached a period of yet bigger public works. The intermittent civil wars were not over, but the army was still under firm central control. For the moment, the call for scapegoats died down. A moment of balance seemed to have arrived. This can only fill a generation like our own, which may be experiencing a similar moment, with interest and apprehension.

On the Christian side, the apologist Athenagoras, in the second century, addressed a pamphlet in the form of a 'supplication' to the Emperor. It was written in a conservative and placatory spirit that emphasized how the Christians were close to the best of the Stoic moral philosophers, and wished to further the pacific and harmonious operation of society. In some ways it was not too far from the anti-Christian writer, Celsus. Athenagoras was not alone in this deference to power: other Christian contemporaries shared it.

Christians with good training in Greek oratory had appeared in the first generation of converts, though not among those responsible for writing of the Gospels. In the second century able Christian literary apologists, trained in philosophy as well in rhetoric, began to tackle the Jewish question from their own point of view. The main manner in which Jewish scriptures were related to Christ by the apologists was through the allegorical method. Adam foreshadowed Christ in a manner that could be described as his providing the 'type' of Christ. Where Old Testament prophecy did not directly predict Christ and his life and doctrine, it foreshadowed it in a general way similar to that in which the Jewish Exodus from Egypt prefigured the redemption brought by Christ the Messiah, or Jonah swallowed and disgorged by the fish became the symbol of the Resurrection.

This allegorical 'typology' has remained one of the main Christian ways of looking at the Jewish scriptures, as anyone may check who looks at the marginal notes of a King James or a Revised version of the Bible. Not unnaturally, the allegations by Christian writers that they understood the true meaning of Jewish scripture in a manner inaccessible to the Jews themselves, were not too kindly received by Jewish scholarship.

Marcion and the Old Testament

One route not followed by mainstream Christianity, but nonetheless important and widely received among second-century Christians, was that of total rejection of Jewish scripture. This was the position of Marcion (c.AD100–c.165), the son of a bishop from Asia Minor, although he preached in Rome. An enthusiast, in his own way, for the doctrines of

Below: A second-century Roman wedding ceremony. The social bonds of family and kinship were immensely important and a significant focus for early Jesus-followers.

St Paul, Marcion saw inconsistency and weakness in the Old Testament accounts of Yahweh. The God of the Old Testament seemed to him a God utterly unacceptable, for the way he occasionally admitted ignorance about his own creation, for his having taken responsibility for the entrance into the world of evil, and for afterwards tolerating that it should continue. The Old Testament, Marcion concluded, should be entirely rejected. By his time, the acceptance of one category (or canon) of authoritative writings about Christian ways to salvation, and the elimination of others, had become a normal practice, although Marcion's wholesale repudiation of the main body of Jewish scripture did not find general favour.

Marcion was also repelled and disgusted by the sexual and reproductive processes that God had determined for men and women. For the numerous Marcionite communities he decreed that marriage and sexual contacts were to be avoided. Marcion emphasized all the elements of the Gospels that were most hostile to the ties of kinship: in ancient society, and also in most societies that followed, down to a comparatively recent time, this was a profoundly disruptive message. Most ancient men saw in kinship the most profound and meaningful of all social bonds. That this was so had already been demonstrated in Christianity in the way the earliest Jesus-follower assembled around the nucleus of his family.

Gnosticism

The desire to find a road to enlightenment and salvation was common to huge numbers of people in the ancient world at this time. It was so not merely for Christians and Jews and their sub-sects, but also for very many, principally mystically inclined, pagans. The Mithraic mysteries, in which ritual meals celebrated the slaying of a primal bull, had an enormous following throughout the Empire, and its adepts had included at least one emperor. The Christians had an idea of individual redemption and of its proximate achievement through God's kingdom that was shared by few; but the notion of enlightenment through revealed knowledge (gnosis) was common to many. The first sentence of the Gospel of John shows that the Christians also followed

Above: A detail from a sarcophagus showing Adam and Eve. For the Christian Gnostic Marcion, sexual activity was abhorrent even though it was a process determined by God for humans.

47

Right: Mithraeum or shrine to Mithras. In Persian mythology, Mithras was said to have slain a bull from whose blood all life sprang. The cult of Mithras was especially popular with the Roman army.

© Ronald Sheridan, Ancient Art & Architecture Collection

this path, and indeed, although 'Gnostic' became a term later applied to certain deviant Christians, it was earlier a designation that some orthodox Christians applied to themselves: a notable example was Clement, a learned and eloquent philosopher and theologian who lived and taught in Alexandria at the end of the second century. The way in which Clement discussed Gnosticism, in spite of the strictures he made concerning one or two individual Gnostic thinkers, showed admiration and respect.

Did Gnosticism exist before Christianity? The historian, Henry Chadwick, has posed the question as follows:

'Were the second-century heresies the consequence of trying to impose alien theosophical elements on the Christian substratum? OR systems which resulted from fitting bits of Christianity into a prior religious entity, which might take several different forms and could assimilate Mithras or Attis or Judaism with as little trouble as it accepted Jesus?'[1]

Gnostic tradition was a complicated mixture, in which the Platonic idea of the immortality of the soul was only one of a number of elements. Faith and wisdom inspired the Gnostic with knowledge of the origin and destiny of the world. Material things were of no concern to the deity, and the all-important element to the believer was the spark of the divine that he carried — if he was one of the enlightened — within him. Such views were ultimately fatal to the sacramental view of material things that lay behind most of the developing sacred drama of the Christian liturgy — one need only think of the prescriptions for baptism that are described above. They were bound, also, to impinge upon people's concepts of a Jesus who had been seen after his death, apparently restored to the condition of an approachable human being.

The Gnostics thought that people had become alienated from the all-informing divine spirit in some original, cosmic disaster, and that only a chosen few could now benefit from the knowledge of their true origin and from their relationship to the divine. Such views had been current in Palestine at the time of the first Jesus-followers; even at this stage there had been a current of Jewish Gnosticism.

In Samaria a preacher called Simon, who probably held Gnostic views, had represented himself as the voice of 'the Great Power'. Simon was given baptism by Philip the Jesus-evangelist, although his proffer of money for authority to 'lay on hands' caused Peter to eject him from the Jesus-community.

How the basic split between the material and the spiritual worlds should determine conduct was a question answered differently by the different Gnostic groups. A majority followed the path attributed to Marcion, and chose to lead extremely ascetic lives, and to refuse or drastically restrict sexual activity. But others decided that, because of the non-divine nature of the material world, as long as they were enlightened adepts of the divine way, it did not matter how their bodies were used; such views could lead to sexual libertinism. There may have been influence of this kind upon the Christian communities at a very early stage and within the lifetime of Paul: something of the kind seems to be hinted at in his letters to the Corinthians.

Zoroastrianism and Manichaeism

The cosmic dualism professed by the Gnostics may eventually have been rooted in Persian (Iranian) Zoroastrianism, which had already in the past influenced Judaism, and had probably been responsible for

Above: Fourth-century Gnostic writings inscribed on stone stele or slabs.

the belief in Satan and in demonic possession that had played a part in the life and ministry of Jesus. But after Zoroaster by far the most influential of the Persian dualisms that grew from Christianity, and proceeded to make inroads on Christians and non-Christians alike, from China through to Mesopotamia, Syria, Egypt, North Africa and Spain, was Manichaeism, the religion that grew from the visions of a Persian Baptist Christian called Mani, born in the province of Media in Mesopotamia. In the early third century Mani was granted a vision of his own Heavenly Twin, or guardian angel, a prelude to the revelations of divine wisdom that followed, one of which showed his opponents sinking for eternity into a black sea.

Mani claimed to be an apostle of Jesus and proclaimed him as a divine being who could not have suffered true incarnation or true death. Like him, Mani worked miraculous feats of exorcism and healing. Like the other Gnostics, Manichaeans supposed an eternal opposition of spiritual light and gross matter. Like them, they made the superior adepts into an God-chosen elite, who in the Manichae case practised severe asceticism, teetotalism and vegetarianism, and even felt it necessary to

Below: Breaking the Bread. Christians celebrating the Eucharist from the catacomb of Priscilla in Rome. The bread and wine symbolized the body and blood of Christ.

Right: Zoroastrian fire altar from Sassanian Persia. Zoroastrianism focused on the struggle between good and evil, predicting the ultimate triumph of good, in the form of the supreme god Ahura Mazdah, often represented as fire.

discourage gardening and silviculture, and to apologize to the bread they consumed – an attitude which has earned for them the contempt of a modern, garden-loving English historian, Robin Lane-Fox. The lesser believers were excused the obligations of chastity and asceticism, but had in compensation to suffer several incarnations before they could be purified to the necessary degree of enlightenment. Like many other Gnostics, the Manichaeans were willing to give women a prominent part in their ceremonies.

Manichaeism gave third- and fourth-century orthodox Christianity a powerful and widespread opposition to contend with, though it was then only one among many Gnostic oppositions. It was destined to endure in various forms for many centuries. Its last conspicuous manifestation in the West was perhaps the Cathar heresy of the twelfth and thirteenth centuries, bloodily put down by the centralized and authoritarian Roman Church of the time.

Orthodoxy, Rite and Ritual

The idea of orthodox Christianity, of a 'great Church' (or 'great assembly', a Jewish idea) that was the God-given custodian of right views about the faith, took root in the second century, in the climate created by the growth of what were seen as a perilous undergrowth of mistaken opinions and customs. Such reactions were already visible in the church of Peter and Paul, in apostolic and following times.

The assertion of right opinion was joined with the assertion of correct and traditional rites, which had been passed down faithfully from earlier times. The rite of baptism has already been described. In the mid-second century the apologist, Justin, described the eucharistic rite that in some ways resembled the order followed in the synagogue, but in others was entirely Christian.

'Bread and a cup of water and mixed wine are brought to the president of the brethren, and he, taking them...offers thanksgiving..'; the administration of the elements to the congregation by the deacons follows. 'This food we call Eucharist, of which no one is allowed to partake except one who believes that the things we teach are true, and has received the washing for forgiveness of sins and for rebirth, and who lives as Christ handed down to us.'

Orthodoxy (correct belief) stands out in every phrase of this account. Those who held these right opinions were the defenders of the great Church that was already widely defined as 'catholic', meaning universal. 'Catholic' was used to serve, as it were, as the Christian surname. When Pionius, a well-educated Christian of Smyrna, was interrogated by the magistrate during the Decian persecution, about what church he was, he replied: 'Of the catholic church, for Christ has no other.'

Irenaeus (AD130–200), the Greek-speaking Bishop of Lyons, the friend and disciple of Bishop Polycarp of Smyrna, was one of the main builders of intellectual defensive systems against what were seen as hostile opinions that threatened the truth of the Gospel messages transmitted to his generation by faithful believers. His main literary work was entitled *Against all Heresies*. In it he took the position that true Christian belief, whose best custodians he thought to be those churches founded by apostles (he cited Rome as a particularly authoritative example), was in effect revealed progressively to faithful persons. The hostility of Irenaeus to curiosity and innovation in religion may make him seem an authoritarian defender of a monolithic 'great Church', but this definition today contains overtones of power and authority that Irenaeus certainly did not possess.

The question of authority led inevitably to that of the authority of texts. It was a question that the Gnostics themselves had also raised, but their criteria were entirely unacceptable to Irenaeus. For example, some Gnostics had their own version of the Gospel, the so-called Gospel of Thomas, the doubting disciple, whose text has been rediscovered only in the present century. 'Gospels' of this kind were rejected by Irenaeus from what came gradually to be known as the canon of accepted sacred writings; some rejected works we still know in the form in which they were consigned to the Biblical Apocrypha. Irenaeus laid great stress upon the joint authority of the four Gospels that were from the following century onwards to be described as 'canonical'. The first systematic list of canonical books in the Old and New Testaments was given by a Council held in Rome in AD 382.

Quarrels started at the very beginnings of the Church, whose history, as the great historian Gibbon spitefully recorded over two centuries ago, is from one point of view one of ceaseless internal hostilities. That these negative elements are not the most basic facts of church history, does not make them go away. Like all scriptural religions, Christianity has its gatekeepers. But for this a price has to be paid. If we can only know about the faith through a tradition that requires interpreters, conflict among the gatekeepers is inevitable.

Persecutions began again in the first half of the third century. One of the triggers for the outbreak was the unsatisfactory Christian attitude to the celebration of Rome's millennium in AD 248, a moment in which loyalty to Roman tradition became politically very sensitive. There had already been a revival

Right: The four tetrarchs: Diocletian, Maximian, Constantius and Galerius. Towards the end of his rule, Diocletian divided the Roman Empire into four political units, two eastern, two western. He and Maximian ruled the east as Augusti; Constantius and Galerius ruled the west as Caesars.

of persecution in AD 235–236, as a reaction against the Emperor Alexander Severus (AD 205–235), who had been seen as excessively pro-Christian. This outbreak may have stimulated the learned controversialist, Origen (AD185–254), to write an exhortation to martyrdom. Origen was an Alexandrian intellectual said to have made himself a eunuch to reduce sexual temptation in the course of giving mixed seminars, a procedure unlikely to recommend itself to modern academics. He was the son of a Christian martyr, and was himself to suffer torture and grievous imprisonment for the faith. However, his 'Exhortation', written before his own arrest and witness, contains a hint of divine threat to the torturers, when he says that the cry of the blood of the martyrs calls to God from the soil on which it fell.

Organization and Infrastructure

However, from AD 260 until the end of the century there was a very important lull in persecution. The Christians all over the Empire benefited from a *de facto* toleration. In spite of the shaky legal basis on which the churches were allowed to own property, many churches were built as public buildings to

Below: The dove of peace hovers above the heads of three youths enduring in the fiery furnace of Nebuchadnezzar (Daniel:3). Detail from fresco in the catacomb of Santa Priscilla, Rome.

accommodate congregations. An elaborate organization of church officials was set up in the richer dioceses to administer charities and relief works. In AD 251 the Roman church had a staff of more than 250 persons, and looked after more than 1500 widows and poor people. Christians were allowed to occupy important public offices, and where these meant executing duties of deference to pagan gods, the authorities were often willing to turn a blind eye. A bishop such as Cyprian of Carthage – who eventually suffered martyrdom – had been a rich and powerful member of the civic magnate class. When toleration returned, many other bishops were accorded respect by the local government authorities.

Diocletian and the Great Persecution

The second half of the third century was, however, a bad time for the Empire. There was recession, inflation, and defeat in some of the great wars on the Roman frontiers. Great soldier-emperors again took control, above all Diocletian (reigned AD 284–305). Towards the end of his long reign, he became worried about the high positions held by Christians in the army. He and one of his junior co-Emperors were incited against them by the Oracle of Apollo at Didyma, near Miletus on the coast of Asia Minor. There had been a remarkable revival in the activities and popularity of the pagan oracles of Asia Minor in the second and third centuries, and Diocletian's visit to Didyma – on which Constantine, the future Christian emperor, may have accompanied him as a young staff officer – witnessed its last big manifestation. Pagan intellectuals were also calling for action against the Christians, notably Porphyry, a pupil of the great Platonist philosopher, Plotinus. The Christians had become vulnerable to official attack, not only for the old ideological and popular reasons, but also because the government had become worried by the power their members held.

On 23 February AD 303, the day of the gods of Boundaries (Terminalia), Diocletian launched one of the final, and perhaps the greatest, of the persecutions. Christians were not only required to submit and sacrifice, but, as in some previous persecutions, also to hand over their sacred books for destruction. This produced divisions among the Christians, because the consignment of the books by the traditores (whose description supplies the origin of the later words for 'traitor') created a new class of apostates whom some Western Christians refused to receive back into the fold when persecution ended. It had previously been accepted that only sacrifice to the pagan gods created an apostasy that was difficult to purge.

Diocletian's persecution was an extremely serious and bloody business, the more serious because the Christians were no longer insignificant scapegoats, but an influential minority, and in some parts of the Empire an influential majority. They no longer met only in poky back rooms, but in substantial churches. The cathedral of Nicomedia was clearly visible from the Emperor's palace. Because of the geographical division of power among the co-Emperors, the effect of the persecutions varied in different parts of the Empire. In the areas subject to Diocletian and Galerius, which included Rome, Syria, Egypt and Asia Minor, all places where the Christians were socially influential and demographically numerous, the persecution was most consistent. It was also savage in North Africa. The Christians were no longer, when suffering the final penalties, always subjected to the jeers of the mob as they had been a generation earlier, but their punishments were still very often ferocious.

I H. Chadwick, *The Early Church* (Harmondsworth, 1967), p. 35

Roman Emperor from AD 284–305, Diocletian launched one of the last and bloodiest of the Christian persecutions.

4

THE CHRISTIAN EMPIRE

In AD 312, Constantine, the joint ruler of the Roman Empire in the west, had a vision. Its impact on the development and spread of Christianity was immeasurable.

Constantine is one of the most difficult major figures in Christian history to assess. It is possible to think of Christian history up to his times in terms of men and women who almost all aspired to holiness, even if they did not all achieve it. But Constantine was a man of power, whose whole life was dedicated to defending and seizing power, who lived behind the mask that all men of power wear, never revealing his motives unless and until it was politically expedient to do so. There are many reasons to believe that he accepted the Christian faith more or less as it was presented to him by its exponents, and that he accepted a duty to serve its aims, especially in supporting its bishops. He accepted without demur the obligation to judge between the quarrelling and disputing members of its clergy. But certainty about his motives seems impossible to obtain.

Constantine had been proclaimed an Augustus in AD 306 at York in Britain, in succession to his father Constantius. Neither was a Christian, but Constantine inherited a tolerant policy towards the Christians from his father, and reinforced this tolerance immediately on his accession by restoring the rights and property Christians had enjoyed before the beginning of the recent persecutions. For another six years, there was no indication that Constantine was getting ready to make the Christian faith the fulcrum of his policies.

Above: The head from the colossal statue of Constantine which once stood in his basilica in Rome.

Left: Scenes from the Passion of Christ on a fourth-century Christian sarcophagus. On the left is the chi-rho symbol that inspired Constantine.

Even after a commitment to Christianity first appeared in AD 312, the translation of this commitment into coherent government policies could not take place until AD 324, when, after conquering his opponent Licinius, Constantine ruled the whole Roman world. To turn the religious policies of a world power upside-down, repudiating the whole former religious basis of the state, could not be effected until the ruler's legitimacy was unquestioned throughout his empire.

Constantine invaded Italy at the beginning of AD 312, and arrived outside Rome in the autumn to confront Maxentius, the other ruler of the western Empire, who was at this stage his main opponent. Maxentius, on his part, was too nervous of internal opposition in Rome to face a siege, and prepared to leave the city with his army, to battle with Constantine on the northern bank of the Tiber, on the Via Flaminia outside the Milvian Bridge.

Below: The Victory of Constantine at the Battle of the Milvian Bridge, a fresco by Piero della Francesca, probably painted in 1452–57. This is part of the True Cross Cycle in the Church of San Francesco, Arezzo, Italy.

A Dream and a Vision

A vision and a dream shortly before the battle determined Constantine on the more or less Christian symbolism to which he should entrust his fortunes. The vision was not his alone but that of his whole army. As they arrived outside Rome they saw a cross, or something very like it, in the noonday sky. The dream was the emperor's alone. In it he saw a sign that he ought to paint on the battle equipment of his troops, in sign of victory. It was not a recognized Christian symbol. The two Greek letters that seem to have composed it, *chi-rho*, could conceivably be understood as the initial letters of *chrestos*, for Christ, although that was a far from obvious interpretation. The sign was, nevertheless, duly inscribed on Constantine's own helmet and on the shields of his personal bodyguard, and in Constantine's view it brought him, together with the symbol of the cross in the sky, a great victory. Maxentius' army was crushingly defeated, and pushed into the Tiber, which flowed at its rear; Maxentius himself drowned with the rest, and Constantine entered Rome as senior Augustus.

What happened in October AD 312 was interpreted by Constantine as a divine dispensation of some kind in his favour. This would have been the conclusion of any earlier emperor; the difference lay in Constantine's decision that it was the God of the Christians who had supported him. He used the *chi-rho* symbol on a new dynastic battle-standard, the so-called 'labarum', which also bore the pictures of Constantine and his children. From that moment Constantine's religious policy was thrown entirely on the Christian side. Towards the official pagan symbolism of Rome he showed at best an ambiguously silent attitude, that after several years changed into outright public rejection. The triumphal arch built for him after he entered Rome still stands just outside the modern Forum area. It contains no central representation of a pagan god. The Senate's inscription on the arch refers to his victory having

© Forum, Rome, Italy/Bridgeman Art Library, London

'...at about midday, when the sun was beginning to decline, he saw with his own eyes the trophy of a cross of light in the heavens above the sun, and bearing the inscription Conquer by This (Hoc Vince). At this sight he himself was struck with amazement and his whole army also...' (Eusebius De VC) 1,28

Left: The Arch of Constantine in Rome, built in AD 315 to celebrate the victory over Maxentius.

Below: A detail from Constantine's triumphal arch, showing the sun god Apollo. Diplomatically, Constantine continued to acknowledge the sun god, while transferring his beliefs to Christianity.

© Ancient Art & Architecture Collection

Right: A c. fourth-century mosaic of Christ as a manifestation of the sun god from the new 'basilica' church built by Constantine on the reputed site of St Peter's martyrdom in Rome.

SCALA

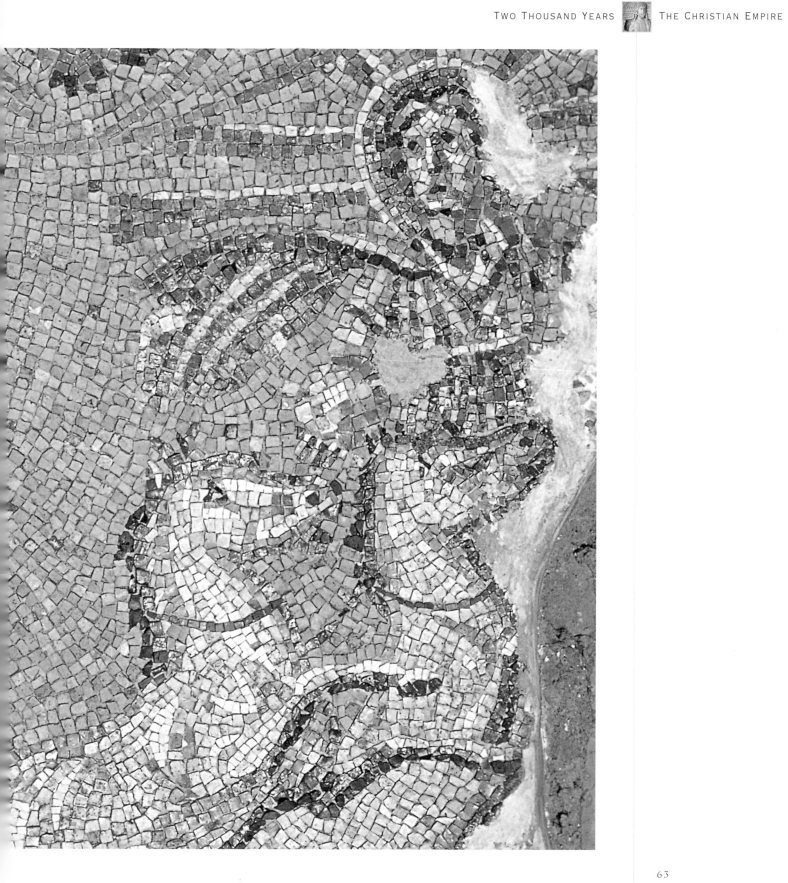

happened 'at the prompting of the deity', by which the sun god may be intended.

The public consequences for Christianity of the Battle of the Milvian Bridge followed quickly and were very favourable. Early in AD 313, Constantine met Licinius, the eastern Augustus, at Milan, and together the two declared a policy of religious tolerance in both parts of the Empire. They purported to think that freedom of worship and the right to care for sacred things according to free choice were individual rights, an unlikely statement of principle for two ruthless autocrats to issue, although one that would have made sense to people of late antiquity.

Constantine's father had been inclined to reverence the sun god, and in the preceding century richer Christians had already employed artists who showed Christ as a sort of manifestation of the sun god. In AD 310, according to a pagan panegyrist, Constantine had had a vision of the sun god Apollo, who offered him crowns to signify his future victories and rule. It is probable, however, that he had understood and accepted the main Christian doctrines soon after AD 312. The Christian Bishop Eusebius wrote of Constantine's talks with Christian apologists, which began immediately after the Battle of the Milvian Bridge. However the overall pagan majority in the Empire was so large that until the victory over Licinius in AD 324, he used the skills of a practised diplomatist and politician to blur the edges of his changes of belief. Continued emphasis on the sun god, which is visible on his coins, may have played a part in this.

The Babylonians, the Assyrians, the Greeks, and especially the small tribe of the Israelites, had all believed that a ruler can owe victory in battle to a god, and in their imagination the divine leader had 'gone before' the warrior king in the battle. Such things can be found in the Old Testament, in Homer and in ancient Mesopotamian writings. If there was ever a religious conversion of Constantine to Christianity, the point of departure must have been something of this ancient nature. Subsequently, when he frequented and consulted Christian holy men, Constantine internalized the Christian moral universe to a high degree: whether this was exceptional among educated converts it is hard to say, but the political stakes for which he had chosen to play in accepting Christianity were extremely high. It is known that he possessed at least the sort of literary culture that would have been expected of a Roman aristocrat, which enabled him to make sense of the disputed Christian theologies of his day.

From his first accession to his father's dominions, Constantine had shown favour to Christians. Apart from having ended the persecution several years before the Battle of the Milvian Bridge, he had already had Christian bishops in his entourage before AD 312. The more bishops he met, the more he understood that skilled and useful propagandists and politicians could be found among them. The presence of numerous and powerful Christian populations in the east of the Empire was an important political factor, when the now aggressively Christian Constantine decided to dispute the Empire with the eastern Augustus.

The decisive year was AD 324. After his fleet had won a big naval battle, Constantine landed his army, achieved decisive victory outside Chalcedon (on the Asian shore of the Bosphorus) over Licinius, the eastern Augustus (and also Constantine's brother-in-law), and made himself sole Roman Emperor. The joint rule of several Augusti that Diocletian had set up, late in the preceding century, was finished, and a single autocrat once more governed the Empire. The new regime was stamped by an ideology of stunning novelty: a lame observance of some of the old rites of the Roman state persisted, but Christianity was to be its official religion.

Above: A gold coin from the reign of Constantine (c. AD 274–337). The labarum can be seen on top of the Imperial standard.

© The Bridgeman Art Library, London

Christianity Established

Constantine's decision to give preference to Christianity appears to have been taken very soon after the Battle of the Milvian Bridge. The first tax exemptions for Christian clergy were made in AD 313, and further ones followed after AD 325. The first of Constantine's huge grants of money for the rebuilding and finance of the major Roman churches also followed quite closely upon the battle. After AD 324, Constantine built a vast new 'basilica' church on the Vatican hill, the reputed site of St Peter's martyrdom. Inside the church he had a splendid monument or Memoria built, to replace the earlier one over the site venerated as that of Peter's tomb. The basilica was one of the standard architectural forms for a major public building in any city centre: the secular basilica built by Constantine in the Roman forum is still partly extant, as is a huge monumental head of Constantine that was probably sited within it.

So, within little more than two and a half centuries, the Emperor honoured in Rome the executed Galilean apostle, whose original tomb – possibly located in the street of late Roman tombs that still

Below: Mosaic pavement from the late fifth century showing a Christian basilica. The basilica design was originally used for secular buildings but was appropriated by Constantine and formed the template for later Christian churches.

Below: A row of columns are all that remains of the Temple of Jupiter, supreme god of the Romans, in the Lebanon. After AD 324, Constantine waged war on pagan temples, describing them as 'groves of falsehood'.

exists under St Peter's – had been probably recorded by no more than a couple of bricks, if it had been marked at all. Other huge Christian basilicas were built by Constantine and his family in Rome and in Palestine. In Rome he built the great new church of St John Lateran, which was the parish church of Rome. It formed part of a huge complex that included a baptistery, a palatial residence for the bishop and appropriate charitable annexes.

Whether financed by the government or other means, churches that had been destroyed in the persecutions all over the Empire were rebuilt. The church in the old eastern capital city of Nicomedia, that had been destroyed at the orders and in the presence of Diocletian himself, was extravagantly reconstructed by Constantine. In Antioch he began to build another great church 'of concord' to replace the old – although, in spite of its title, its dedication in AD 341, four years after the death of Constantine, was accompanied by an almighty theological row among the clergy.

Constantine's hostility to paganism was now open; he described the temples as 'groves of falsehood'. Although pagan beliefs were not in themselves made illegal, many of the institutions that supported pagan worship were in effect proscribed, and sacrifice, the essence of the cults, was forbidden. The temples were not systematically destroyed, but their funds and valuable possessions were expropriated (with the exception of worship forming part of the state religion, which continued under the emperor who was its chief priest or *pontifex maximus*). A large part of the former resources of the pagan temples was in effect reallocated to Christian churches, and permanent government subsidies were set up for the latter. Certain sexually immoral cults were proscribed, such as that practised in the northern hills of Lebanon at Aphaca at the source of the river of Adonis (now Nahr Ibrahim), and the temples razed. Ferociously puritanical laws about conduct in sexual matters were enacted. Men guilty of rape or abduction were to be burned alive (as were consenting girl victims), and women servants who abetted abduction were to swallow boiling lead. This was not a gradualist emperor who was slowly educating the pagan people in a kinder way of life, but an autocrat of whom the modern mirror image would be the Communist Russian governments which imposed atheism after the Revolution. Like the Communists, Constantine allowed a semblance of the old religion to continue, and like them, he had paid lip service to religious toleration.

Constantine's savage laws reflected tendencies that were to be found, though in a much milder form, in the churches. The need to combat the 'encratic' or sex-renouncing doctrines of many Gnostic teachers had now declined, and the practice of virginity and widowhood dedicated to God was generally encouraged. The idea of 'brides of Christ' began to be spoken of. Women became hermits, undertook long pilgrimages, possessed a means of withdrawal to some extent from the closed world of the family. These were not all negative things. Holy women were privileged, and one of the ways they could use this privilege was to have close spiritual relationships with other holy women or men. Rich holy women could also set up convents that made them in effect into influential church dignitaries.

Left: An early Christian cleric from the Lullingstone fresco of the fourth century. As the officially recognized state religion, Christianity by this time had become formalized and ordered into bishoprics with a hierarchy of administrative staff.

Constantine did not become a Christian in the full sense until he was baptized on his death-bed in AD 337; in this he was only following a very common practice. This did not mean that the emperor, who was sometimes styled by his bishops as 'equal of the apostles' did not accept to the full his responsibility for the unity and discipline of the Christian Church he supported. Fourth-century church leaders quarrelled and bickered endlessly about the ways in which their faith ought to be defined: some of these disagreements were technical or linguistic, but others went to the core of the faith.

Right: The First Council of Nicaea, a fresco by Speranza dating from about 1600. At this momentous Council, called by Constantine himself in AD 325 to resolve the Arian controversy, the exact wording of the Creed was established. This defined what orthodox Christians believed to be the nature of the relationship between Jesus Christ and God.

© AKG London

Power to the Bishops

By the fourth century, church leadership was exercised without serious contest by the bishops. The antiquity and apostolic connections of the various bishoprics had an important influence on the authority and credit given their various incumbents. Each of the ancient sees felt itself particularly responsible for the transmission of authentic doctrine and practice. In the west, there was no serious competitor to Rome, although the status of Milan in Italy and Carthage in Africa was much respected. There was a group of prestigious eastern sees: Jerusalem, Antioch, Alexandria, Nicomedia, Ephesus

and Caesarea are the obvious ones. The inclusion of Nicomedia in this list shows that the Roman provincial system was not without influence on the way that churchmen thought of their bishops.

There was a persistent problem: under what circumstances could Christians who had compromised with the persecutors in order to survive be accepted back into communion after the storms had passed? In North Africa, these uncertainties had produced the 'Donatist' schism. In AD 314, when his engagement with Christianity was absolutely fresh, Constantine summoned a meeting of Christian bishops from the west of the Empire to Arles, near Vienne on the lower Rhone, to try to deal with the matter.

The Arian Controversy

More challenging to Constantine as an arbitrator were the disputes concerning the nature of Christ that were rocking the churches of the East, and that required early settlement after the victory over Licinius in AD 324. Arius, an Alexandrian priest of impressive ability, also had the gifts of a great popularizer: among other talents, he was able to set his theological verses as popular songs. Arius chose to take up a theological position about Christian definition of the nature of the Godhead that was, at least in appearance, relatively easy to comprehend, and that must be allowed to have raised

Right: A silver casket from the fourth century. This wedding present, from a Roman Christian named Secundus to his wife, indicates how the old pagan gods and the new religion rubbed along together. On the lid of the casket is a scene showing Venus.

© British Museum, London, UK/Bridgeman Art Library, London

legitimate doubts about some of the competing theories. He sustained that if God is one ultimate and self-sufficient principle, and at the same time also three separate beings, there are perhaps insuperable difficulties in saying that the Father and the Son are one indissoluble being, who as the incarnate (and therefore limited) son is nevertheless uncreated, as the father is.

The doctrine of Arius held that Christ must have been in some sense inferior to the Father, and must in some way have had a beginning in time. This was a doctrine entirely different from the types of doctrine professed by the Gnostics, and was a product of the reasoning of the Alexandrian church from which Arius came, particularly the reasoning of the great thinker Origen (that in itself could be sustained as orthodox). Plenty of very respectable Eastern clergy took Arianism, the doctrine of Arius, very seriously, including Constantine's later clerical adviser, Eusebius of Caesarea. However, a local church council in Alexandria condemned Arius, who left Egypt for Asia Minor.

The Solution of Nicaea

It may be that Constantine saw Arius and his doctrine as primarily an administrative problem, caused by a cleric who was unnecessarily rocking the boat. He certainly took his own responsibility to the Divinity for the welfare of the churches of the Empire extremely seriously. A Council of Bishops had been summoned in AD 325. Constantine had it transferred to Nicaea (Iznik), the site of an imperial palace. The peace and concord of the church were very important to the emperor, at a moment when he was launching new policies for a reunified Empire that used the Christian religion as their most important principle. The bishops, some two or three hundred of whom attended the council, used the imperial posting service to get to the conference, and their expenses were all government-funded. The bishops had not become part of the Roman civil service, nor were they to do so, but they had become part of the imperial organization in a wider sense.

There had been at least one episode in the third century when bishops in dispute had appealed to the pagan emperor for settlement, but the dispute had not concerned doctrine. The part played by Constantine at Nicaea was an absolute novelty, because he himself formed an integral part of the Church Council, presiding over the opening sessions which took place in the imperial palace. At later sessions he was often present, and without doubt extremely influential. That a Christian still technically under instruction, a so-called catechumen, should be playing a major part in defining the faith, did not, in the imperial circumstances, seem odd. What may seem odd to those who think of the clergy as a learned profession is that a central tenet in the Creed still recited in Christian churches is perhaps the work of an amateur theologian.

This central tenet concerned the description to be used of the common nature of God the Father and God the Son. The relationship was defined by the Council as one of 'identity in being' (*homoousios*, 'of one substance', a suggestion that Eusebius said was due specifically to Constantine himself). To the learned professionals that some of the bishops were, this definition was still somewhat ambiguous, and the ambiguity may well have been apparent to Constantine. But it was a formula of which any diplomat might have been proud, as all but two of the bishops present felt able to adhere to it, and the Council was also able to anathematize Arius – not that this entirely silenced him, or removed his party for ever from the scene. The two bishops who refused to adhere to the anathema against Arius incurred the civil penalty of exile. No one knows what the informal reactions of the bishops to the Council of Nicaea were. But to some of the eldest among them, who a generation earlier had experienced contact with the imperial government in the torture chamber, sitting down with Constantine in the imperial palace at the final state banquet must have been a strange experience.

Nicaea showed that Christian rulers were not going to be neutral in the major disputes of the clergy, and this has remained true to the present day. The peace of the church was far too important for Constantine to leave it entirely to the decisions of a lot of bickering bishops, who had filled his lap with petitions denouncing one another for this cause or that on the very first day of the Council. That he was present merely as an interested Christian observer strains all credulity. The subsequent history of church councils is against it. An early instance of the emperor's direct intervention is that

'For my part, I hold any sedition within the Church of God as formidable as any war or battle, and more difficult still to bring to an end. I am consequently more opposed to it than anything else.' (Constantine's opening address at the Council of Nicaea.)

Right: Detail from a stone block from the Neumagen School Pillar, dating from second to third century AD. When the apostate Emperor Julian reinstated paganism, Christian schoolteachers, who were supposed by Julian to know nothing of the old religion, found themselves redundant.

of AD 359 by Constantine's successor Constantius. He had the bishops meet in two separate councils of East and West in order to get the decision (more or less in favour of Arianism) he wanted over vexed questions that were to some extent a rerun of those discussed at Nicaea. This kind of thing became permanent; if we look forward to the later Roman ('Byzantine') Empire, and then forward again to relatively modern times, say to the sixteenth-century Council of Trent, we find the same phenomenon of lay powers straining every diplomatic nerve to influence theological decisions.

Constantine saw the bishops as leaders of their congregations, whom the imperial autocracy should support, subsidize, revere, and who were formally independent of the state in matters of church discipline, even though he had no hesitation in exercising political pressure to obtain the church policies he wanted. There was both paradox and ambiguity in this relationship. The Christian dialogue with power, which had experienced some periods of calm in the preceding century, but all too often had been one of fear and terror, had entered upon a new phase, one that was wonderfully favourable to the spread of the good news of the Gospel in many respects, but that held dangers of a new kind for the believers.

From AD 324 onwards Christianity became to some extent a prerequisite of imperial favour, though pagan favourites and panegyrists were still not entirely obsolete. The old social and religious structure of the Empire still told against the new religion in many ways. In every city there were dignitaries such as the flamines, urban notables, whose civic functions were inseparable from their pagan religious ones. The entire framework of civic decorum and tradition had a pagan basis and vocabulary that could not disappear overnight.

Julian the Apostate

The concepts of what we would now call high culture were still in some respects foreign to the majority of Christians. The traditional vocabulary of Christian teaching, from the Greek Gospels outwards, was based on what was called in the law courts the *sermo humilis*, meaning that it was expressed in popular idiom. At first, it made only a marginal difference that for a long time the religion had been attracting people of good literary and intellectual attainments, who sometimes had claimed all sorts of pagan literary precedents for Christian ideas, finding them in the pronouncements of the sibyls and the works of Virgil – as Constantine himself had done, in his only known literary composition. But a new Christian Empire was not long in producing a new Christian political vocabulary. Imperial panegyrists emerged who swiftly adapted Biblical concepts of royalty and majesty to the new Roman situation.

The term 'pagan' to describe a non-Christian was unknown to the literate people of classical antiquity until quite a late date. Its primary meaning was to indicate someone who was a civilian as opposed to a soldier: whether this meant, not a 'soldier of Christ', is uncertain. It also had a quite separate meaning of 'rustic' or countryman, which came sometimes to be applied to non-Christians of a rather later date.

By AD 361 Christianity had so far become the dominating orthodoxy of the dynasty of Constantine that the idealistic young Julian, Constantine's great-nephew, who had escaped the massacre of males of the half-blood in AD 337 because of his infancy, could profess paganism and a passionate faith in the old high culture of Rome, particularly in Platonism, as a mark of adolescent rebellion against the tyranny of the elders. When he became emperor in AD 361 Julian formally threw off Christianity, thus gaining for himself the later title of 'Apostate'. That Julian had the political ability and the force to reverse the religious and social revolution due to Constantine seems unlikely.

He failed to see that by his day, if the Empire had a social cement, it was already Christianity. In the event his policy got no further than a declaration of general toleration, followed by the reopening of the temples and the encouragement of pagan cult rites, and a sharp cut in state subsidies to the churches. Schoolteachers, as sometimes occurs in ideological quarrels, were among the innocent victims. Julian argued that people should not teach things, such as pagan literature, of which they did not approve, and so Christian schoolmasters lost their jobs. In general, although he preferred pagans for promotion, Julian consciously avoided anything that could be interpreted as a renewal of the persecutions of Christians.

In the East the Christian mob lost little time in replying with riots, and with the vandalization of the restored temples, but there was never time for a general reckoning, because of Julian's early death in a skirmish on the Persian frontier, in AD 363. Outside a few elitist and culturally conservative circles, particularly in Rome, there seems to have been general relief that the Empire could return to what had become traditional dynastic religious policies, and to observing the latest moves in the theological struggles about Arianism.

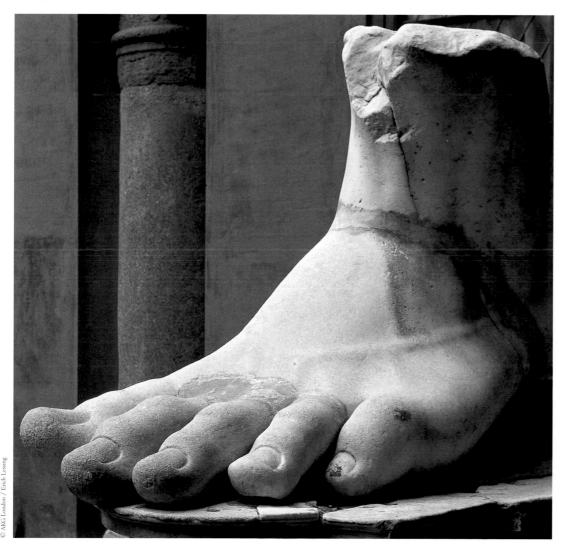

© AKG London / Erich Lessing

Left: The massive left foot from the larger than life statue of Constantine symbolizes the power and autocracy of the man. His vision and adoption of the cross marked a turning point in the fortunes of Christianity.

5

BISHOPS
AND HERMITS

The bishops had become minor political players on the imperial board. The annual cost of the Church to the Empire had come to exceed the cost of the imperial civil service. The ideological results of this degree of commitment by the state can sometimes seem bizarre. The disputes between the clergy concerning the definition of the divine natures was a serious matter for all Christians, but it could be only be expressed in terms that come easier to philosophers than to holy men. The situation was rather as if all today's Western governments had for the past thirty years been compelled, as a part of their main political objectives, to have a policy on structuralism and post-structuralism. Constantinian and post-Constantinian bishops whose policies were later to come to be seen as having been orthodox, could incur severe government displeasure.

For example, under Constantine, Athanasius, the bad-tempered and violent but nevertheless orthodox Bishop of Alexandria, was a fervent and influential supporter of the Nicaean solution of the controversy about the divine natures. Yet he was condemned unjustly for supposedly mistaken doctrines by a packed church council in Tyre in AD 335; he might have secured imperial support, had he not rashly used his position as bishop to threaten to organize a dock strike in Alexandria. He was exiled to Trier on the Rhine frontier and, after Constantine's death, he fled to Rome, where the Roman bishop received him in AD 340. The doctrines of Athanasius were unacceptable at that time to most of the eastern clergy, and also to the imperial court, but he was supported by the popes of the time.

The Athanasius affair was the first of the serious squabbles between Latin west and Greek east: they were to continue spasmodically for another millennium. The disunity of the east and west made Arian influence on the imperial court even more powerful, and Arianism was not finally defeated in the East until a church council held in Constantinople in AD 381. At the same council, a deeply divisive decision was made that the Bishop of Constantinople should rank after the Bishop of Rome, 'because

Left: Renaissance polyptych illustrating, from left to right, Bishops Gregory, Ambrose, Augustine and Jerome.

Above: Relief showing Theodosius I (AD 347–395) and his family. Theodosius was the first emperor to submit to the moral superiority of the Church, when he did public penance before Ambrose in AD 390.

it is new Rome.' The promotion openly placed the politics of the Empire above the traditions of the Church, which gave bishoprics more or less weight and prestige according to their apostolic history.

The Church and the State

Fourth-century bishops lived in a world in which religion had become one of the most powerful, if not the most powerful, agent of social change. From AD 363, under the Emperor Julian's successors, the drift towards Christian conformism gathered momentum. In AD 380 Theodosius (AD 339–97) made Christianity the official religion of the state, and began to initiate severe punitive measures against religious dissidents such as the Manichees. The Church began to be a career for the educated classes. The magnate-bishop had not been unknown – the martyred Cyprian of Carthage was a third-century example – but he began to be a very common phenomenon. Ambrose of Milan, one of the greatest bishops of the period, a man with the power and independence to put the emperor into a penitent's habit, was the son of a praetorian prefect (who was a Christian), and at the time of his election was himself the governor of Aemilia-Liguria, with his seat at Milan. In AD 374 Ambrose, although still unbaptized, was acclaimed bishop. He resisted nomination, and tried to fend it off by immediately having some suspects tortured in a way he hoped would disqualify him for a bishop's office.

Unable to refuse the bishopric, Ambrose became the first bishop to bring the administrative experience of the top echelons of the Empire to the governance of the Church. His influence over the emperors was of major political importance. He was instrumental in securing laws and policies that virtually eliminated Arianism in the Balkans, and that made paganism into something quite close to a proscribed religious attitude. His major clash with the government did not concern his own diocese, but distant Thessalonica, where the Emperor Theodosius in AD 390 had massacred 7,000 innocent persons in the stadium, to punish the city for riots against the government. Ambrose required and obtained that Theodosius should accept excommunication and do penance for the deed. The event did not inaugurate some sort of quasi-theocratic rule: the Empire was too hardy a plant for that. But it showed that the moral order of the Church could now challenge the moral order of the Empire in ways hitherto undreamed of.

Ambrose was the ideal type of the patrician bishop, and with this he united some of the charismatic qualities of the holy man, including an alarming capacity, on occasion, to strike the wicked dead on the spot. The holy-man bishop was not extinct by any means, but he was not welcomed as he might have been a century earlier. In AD 370 neighbouring bishops had objected to the future St Martin of Tours, a Pannonian ex-soldier, as Bishop of Tours on the grounds that he was dirty and unkempt.

Where bishops were not themselves great men, they tended to pay court to the great. This, again, was far from new, but in this period it became far more widespread than hitherto. In Rome, these things had been so for a long time, but the fourth century, a period of immense enrichment of church treasures and possessions, and of the construction of many of the city's greatest churches, saw some quite worldly Roman bishops. When Pope Liberius, whose Roman basilica is still the greatest Roman treasure house of fifth-century art, was exiled as a result of his siding with Athanasius in the Arian dispute, the smart society ladies of Rome petitioned the Emperor for his return.

The Nature of Christ

The early fifth century was a time of ferocious theological quarrels about the elements of man and God in the person of Jesus. The disputes were politicized because of the involvement of the emperors and their families, and they aroused the passions of whole populations in the eastern part of the Empire. Because of the interest of the Empire in compelling some sort of settlement, in 451 the main

Above: Illuminated manuscript from the fifteenth century, made for the Duke of Burgundy, showing St Martin of Tours.

theological questions were compromised in the Council of Chalcedon (situated on the Bosphorus). The Council said that Jesus was fully God and fully man in both his natures, consubstantial with God the Father as regards his deity, and of the same substance as men, as regards his humanity.

About the theological disputes of this 'sad century', a wise church historian of an earlier generation may be quoted:

> 'Since... ...the unwisdom of the theologians kept upon the dissecting table the Sweet Saviour who offered Himself for our love and our imitation far more than for our philosophical investigations, at the least it was requisite that these should be conducted in a peaceable manner by men of acknowledged competence and distinction, far aloof from the crowd and its bickerings. It was the contrary that happened.'[1]

There remained after Chalcedon a contested distinction between those who said that Christ was in two natures, and those said he was from two natures. The dispute became a clash of cultures between the Egyptian-Syrian part of the Empire and Constantinople, that was finally to be rendered obsolete by the Arab generals of Muhammad in the mid-seventh century. Theological hates therefore still flourished: only six years later a Patriarch of Alexandria was lynched and murdered by the populace in order to let in a bishop who satisfied the local dislike of the theologians of Constantinople.

The controversies about the divine and human in the person of Christ had results that may not all be obvious to modern people. One of the most passionate opponents of Arius, Apollinaris of Laodicea (d. AD 390), emphasized the incarnation of the divine word in Christ to such a point that Jesus appears not to have had, in his view, a mind that was truly human, but rather one that was divine. Mary was thus literally Theotokos, God-bearer or mother of God. A very popular devotion to Mary already existed, but her status as Virgin Mother was enormously increased by this new theological twist, that attributed the most basic of all ties of kinship to the deity himself.

Above: Detail from a third-century fresco from the catacombs of Priscilla, in Rome, showing the Virgin Mary as Theotokos, or God-bearer.

Right: The remains of the baptistry in the church of the Virgin Mary at Ephesus, southern Turkey. It was here that the third Ecumenical Council was held in 431.

The orthodox theologians on the whole repudiated Apollinaris, but they could not stop the drift towards the veneration of Mary, who had accepted the invitation to bear the Christ-child, which had been offered her by the angel of God. Another theologian suspected of rationalism was the Patriarch of Constantinople, Nestorius, who had created scandal by remarking that 'God is not a baby two or three months old.' Nestorius was judged at the Council of Ephesus in 431, his condemnation took place in one of the first Christian churches to be dedicated to Mary, and the final statement of the Council referred to the union of two natures in Christ, 'on which ground we confess Christ to be one, and Mary to be the mother of God.' In Rome, too, the great basilica built by Pope Liberius in the preceding century was dedicated to Mary (the basilica of St Mary Major), and Pope Sixtus III (432–440) decorated it lavishly with mosaics, some of which are still in place, that honour Mary the God-bearer.

Sin, Guilt and St Augustine

One of the greatest of the fifth-century bishops, Augustine, Bishop of Hippo (Bône in Algeria; he had been born in Thagaste, in the interior, now Souk Ahras, in AD 354), was great in his own times,

Above: A sixth-century mosaic from Carthage, showing a Vandal on horseback, leaving his villa. Having invaded north Africa, the Vandals set up their capital at Carthage where they adopted a Roman lifestyle.

Left: The Vision of St Augustine painted by the Venetian artist Vittore Carpaccio (c. 1450–1522). Initially a Manichaean, Augustine was baptized in AD 387 and became Bishop of Hippo in Algeria.

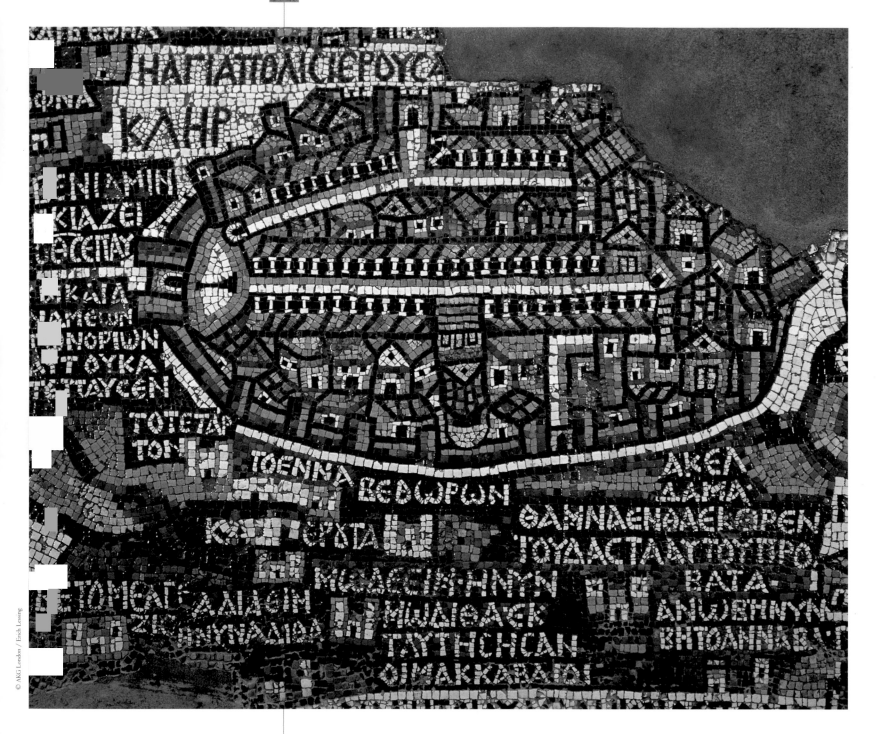

© AKG London / Erich Lessing

Above: Detail from a sixth-century mosaic map of Palestine and Egypt, built into a modern church in Madaba, Jordan, and showing Jerusalem with its Constantinian buildings.

but even more remarkable for the immense influence that he exerted on later times. Augustine was not a patrician bishop: he was, on the contrary, an example of the promotion that skilful men of letters could still obtain in late antiquity, coming from modest families quite outside the official world. Tragically, he who had lived through so many of the dramas of his times, survived to die in his own cathedral city, while it was under under siege from the Vandal armies (Christian, but heretical and Arian) that were sweeping through North Africa. Hippo was to fall in 431, a year after his death, and the rest of Roman Africa with it.

In the rustic outpost of Thagaste, and later in Carthage, the young Augustine learned enough of the classics to lay the basis for a later literary career, though not enough to give him a good knowledge of Greek. This was a limiting factor, because the big theological debates in Augustine's lifetime over doctrines of the divine natures were almost all conducted in Greek. As a bishop, Augustine was the correspondent of a few of the great Christian figures of his period, such as St Jerome, the Jerusalem-based author of the Latin 'Vulgate' translation of the Bible, and Paulinus of Nola, but he had no direct contact with the theologians of the east.

The great originality of Augustine was to understand the historical situation of Christianity, at a moment when a large part of the political and social structure of the western Empire was collapsing. The Roman army, on which the Empire depended to remain in being, did not entirely disappear. But in the south, the north and the west of the Empire, and also for a long time in Rome and the Italian peninsula, the capacity of the army to defend the interior was so diminished that the basic Roman administrative structures became hardly recognizable. The towns, which had been the core of the protected Roman area, and had frequently been based on the great military camps, suffered severely. In Gaul, in Spain, Roman culture was to a considerable extent taken over by barbarian, sometimes heretic nobilities, who then co-existed with the survivors of the old, provincial elites. At the peripheries, in Roman Britain, on the Danube, and in Africa outside Egypt, recognizable Roman rule ceased to exist.

The responsibility that fell upon the Church tended to dominate Augustine's life as a bishop in a practical as well as in a general way. Ever since the Christianization of the Empire, bishops had become part of the system of patronage and favour that governed all late Roman elites. They sat in judgement upon endless lawsuits, and were endlessly asked to favour the promotion of this person or that, or beseeched to influence the outcome of lawsuits in which they were not judges. These things would have been so whether Roman administration was being transformed under 'barbarian' pressure or not. But behind all this, especially after the signals conveyed by the temporary but destructive occupation of Rome by the barbarian Alaric's troops in 410, lay the rapid deterioration of the whole political system. Such things inspired Augustine to remark that:

'We (the Church) are having to conduct the affairs of a whole people — not of the Roman people on earth, but of the citizens of the Heavenly Jerusalem.'[2]

St Augustine marks the point at which the Church ceased to be the gathered church of the faithful few: the people who by temperament wanted to belong to such groups were in his time creating new locations and vocations within the Church, where they might feel more at home. In his book, *The City of God* (413–26), Augustine took a considered, deliberate look backwards at the long history of the pagan Empire of Rome, and at the relatively short history of the Christian Empire. As he did so, he not only passed moral judgement on the old Empire, but also formed new theories of political and social life that were consciously adapted to the imperatives of the world in which he lived. The expression 'catholic' meaning universal or all-embracing had been in use since the end of

Right: A scene from the school of Plato, from Pompeii. St Augustine had been a keen student of Platonic thought.

© Roger-Viollet, Paris/Bridgeman Art Library, London

the first Christian century, especially to describe the 'great' or universal Church of orthodox belief, in opposition to mistaken, heretical belief. With Augustine, the expression becomes a decisive way of including the right-thinking, and excluding the rest.

St Augustine was able to look at the pagan Roman Empire with a cold scepticism that had never before been publicly available, to condemn its ruthless *Realpolitik*, and to remark that 'kingdoms are great robberies'. In him the rhetoric of earlier Christian publicists about the providential nature of the pagan Empire, which had provided such a great peaceful field for the sowing of the Gospel, had vanished. But his appreciation of the positive values of pagan thought and culture, and particularly of the Platonism that he had so eagerly studied, was undimmed. It could not have been otherwise, since it was to this culture that he owed the literary sensibility that was the foundation of his being. Nor had Augustine in the least abandoned the typically Roman values of peace and order, which remained at the top of his moral hierarchy. Peace was the one aim that the earthly city and the heavenly city pursued in common, and order was in either case the guarantor of peace.

There is a sort of political dualism in Augustine, which was to endure throughout the Middle Ages in the clerical mentality. The Christian had a kind of double membership of society. In so far as the Christian was a sort of resident alien in the earthly city, he or she accepted its rules so long as they did not go against divine 'eternal' law. But there is only one republic of all Christians, and this land of the heavenly Jerusalem could in one sense be located in this life. It was a concept destined to grow into that of 'Christianity' or 'Christendom'.

Augustine went along with earlier clerical leaders, in asking the state to enforce Church discipline. The African 'Donatists', who had refused to receive back into the Church the 'traditores', who handed over holy books during the persecutions, had for the preceding century run a nonconformist church, electing their own bishops. In 411 there was a conference in Carthage of Catholic and Donatist bishops, in which both sides spoke under the presidency of the imperial commissioner. After a number of sessions the good manners with which the conference had begun ceased, and the meeting turned into a trial in which the commissioner delivered judgement. Relying on the precedent of the appeal of both sides to the Emperor Constantine in AD 314, he gave the Catholic bishops what they asked, and in Augustine's words, 'compelled them to come in'. There was a thorough repression of the Donatists, which dissolved their organization and visited individual membership of their church with penalties. It was an invocation of the secular arm to compel and punish dissent, of a sort that persisted in the Latin Catholic Church until modern times.

The Desert Hermits

St Augustine's world included the African desert, but his sphere of action was essentially urban. In many respects Christianity had, from the beginning, followed the ways of the ancient pagan world, which led from one city to another. But faith could have a very different setting. In the Mediterranean and African lands that gave harbour to the Jewish sects and to early Christianity, there was unplanted wilderness outside the settled and cultivated land. The shepherds of the pastoral folk might wander in the wilderness, but to the cultivators this was a hostile world. The indigent, or those banished for crimes or fleeing punishment, might find themselves there. So also might the holy. In the stories of St John the Baptist and Jesus, of the Essenes, or six centuries later in that of Muhammad, the desert was present as well as the sown land. The holy man, or the man who aspired to holiness, could not always achieve the self-mastery and the communion with God that he sought, through the life of the towns and villages. The claims of kinship alone would impede him, as Jesus himself had complained. In the wilderness the fasting and self-denial that led to holiness had a different meaning than they had in the towns.

There was no theological room in Christianity for people to wander into the desert to seek a new revelation, although the Gnostic initiates may sometimes have pointed in this direction. But in the middle Nile valley, south of Memphis, a pious Christian youth named Antony had found his way to the desert in the late third century AD to escape from the family and other pressures that impeded him from seeking God. Sexual problems may have played a part, although they did not loom as large in his ascetic enterprise as the visual fantasies of Hieronymous Bosch and the

Below: A fourth- or fifth-century image of the 'lady of Carthage', believed to be an African Donatist. She is thought to have instigated Donatism by falling out with the Bishop of Carthage and electing a rival bishopric.

Left: The Mother Figure on the Altar of Peace in Rome, a pagan representation that influenced the imagery of the Madonna. During the fourth century, the status of Mary as Virgin Mother increased enormously.

Right: Present-day Coptic monks at the monastery of St Bishoi, Wadi El Natrun, in the western desert. Monasticism began in the Egyptian desert.

© Sonia Halliday Photographs

literary fantasies of Gustave Flaubert have made them. For much of his long life (he died in AD 356) he was a conspicuous representative of a wide Christian trend. After spending twenty or thirty years as a hermit, Antony moved his life to the eastern desert; by this time his refuges were surrounded by the refuges of other hermit followers. In the same period great new migrations into the desert took place further north, in the Nile Delta at Scetis (Wadi Natrun) and Nitria. Coptic monks still live in or near these places.

John the Baptist had lived in the wilderness dressed in a coat of camel's hair and a leather belt, and had fed there on locusts and wild honey. By the standards of fourth century Egyptian and Syrian asceticism, he had all but feasted. The fasts and vigils of the desert fathers, and their continuous exposure to sun, thirst, cold and all the hazards of a starkly hostile environment, made them into heroes of a new sort. They voluntarily undertook the semi-starvation and privations that were the worst fears of the rustic poor. They sometimes imposed penances upon themselves which appear superfluous, such as loading themselves with heavy chains.

The hermits were privileged in their exemption from the awful responsibilities of maintaining families through times of fear and famine. For these gains, and for the privilege of finding their own way to salvation, they often paid a truly dreadful price. Most were publicly anonymous, although all were treated with reverence by the laity, who judged an audience with one of them a kind of physical

Left: The base of the column of St Simeon the Stylite (AD 390–459) in the courtyard of St Simeon Monastery, Qalat Sim'an.

touching of the eternal. Those who were widely known as holy men lived the same life of austerity, but they were also public figures, who were called upon to adjudicate quarrels and lawsuits, to forward petitions to the government, and to act as consulting pyschiatrists. Their austerities were often trimmed to their public needs. It was to flee the press of suitors and pilgrims that continually surrounded him that Simeon 'Stylites' lived for years at a time perched at the summit of tall stone pillars. His pillars, now contained within the great ruined church of Qalat Sim'an in Syria, were not situated far out in the desert, but a few miles off the main Roman road (a long tract of which still exists) from Antioch to Chalcis.

Below: A sixth-century representation of Simeon Stylites on his pillar. The Devil in serpent form attacks him in an attempt to dislodge the saint.

From a conforming Christian point of view, one objection to the desert was the entire absence of churches, and the practical impossibility of attending the liturgy, and taking part in the communal life of the congregation, except in the most occasional manner. The bishops were leaders of urban communities: there was already difficulty in finding ways of evangelizing the countryside, and the problems of controlling disorderly hermits in a wilderness were not always welcome to them. The Church had already experienced intractable problems in rural areas. For example, the schismatic Donatists in Africa had been far harder to cope with because of their having been supported by wandering rural bands of supporters. One thinks of the recent history during the 1990s of the Taliban movement in Afghanistan, the supreme recent example of the religious dictatorship of country lads.

In one way the development of a sort of communal ascetic life in the desert was inevitable, because the hermits tended to cluster round leaders, and also because of the purely practical advantages of mitigating the rigours of desert life by some sort of loose association. In the fourth century, much further south in the Nile valley, in the Thebais north of Luxor (Tabennisi near present Qina), there emerged a different, more tightly organized kind of community, under a superior called Pachomius. He organized the desert-dwellers into a labouring semi-military organization, something between a modern kibbutz and a medieval monastery.

The movement of the hermits pointed to the permanent tension in Christianity between the solitary seeker after God and the life of the believing community. To what extent was the solitary to be allowed to place the needs of his own spiritual devotion and quest before the needs of others in the fellowship of religion? He made few material demands on the other believers, it is true, but he made moral ones. There were also supposed hermits in the desert who created problems of a quite different sort – bankrupts, people on the run from justice, bandits, who might all claim to shelter under the cloak of religion.

The Roots of Monasticism

A kind of answer to these problems was offered by an eastern intellectual bishop, St Basil, Bishop of Caesarea in Cappadocia (d. c. AD 379). Basil encouraged the growth of communities that were in essence what would later be called monasteries (coenobia) in which religious men lived under a set of accepted rules, worshipped in the context of a common life, and were firmly placed within the control of the local bishop. The bishop occasionally abused his position by using the monks as auxiliary troops or gangs in theological rows with other churchmen. But on the whole Basil's new arrangements, where they were adopted, worked in the direction of peace and order.

A western alternative to the ideas of Basil was produced by a monk from the Danube frontier called Cassian, trained in the eastern Empire, who set up monastic communities of both men and women in Gaul, near Marseilles. The western attitude to these things was on the whole more disciplined than that of the the East. Cassian's regime was essentially one of communal prayer, organized into five daily 'offices' that the monks or nuns executed together. The regime of prayer was supplemented by a regime of labour, either intellectual or physical. The moral control was strict, and the sequestered community was given a kind of programme to try to overcome the sins that monastic management carefully indicated to them. It was the beginning of monastic life organized for the praise of God, to be carried out by ordinary (but dedicated) persons rather than by spiritual heroes.

1 Mons. L. Duchesne, *Early History of the Christian Church*, trs. C. Jenkins, vol. 3 (London, 1924), p. 226

2 Quoted by Peter Brown, *Augustine of Hippo: a biography* (London, 1967), p. 287

6

BARBARIANS, MISSIONARIES AND SAINTS

The barbarians who entered the Roman Empire in late antiquity were far from alien savages. Most had been within the frontiers of the Empire for a considerable period, either as allies or as troops actually serving in the Roman army. A considerable number of the late Roman generals were barbarians, and by the sixth century Roman armies were in most ways like barbarian ones. When barbarians settled within the frontiers, they were usually qualified as 'guests' and the law applied to their presence, making a fictional assumption that it was acceptable to their Roman hosts, was Roman billeting law. Their numbers were not so great that they completely swamped existing local society. In modern terms, most of them could be described as 'assimilated' Romans, even when their tribal law and customs continued to apply in some respects at least. Barbarian notables became part of the same society as the Roman provincial nobility.

However, religion did not fit tidily into this pattern. The Arian missionaries had been extremely active on the northern borders, especially on the Danube frontier, and some of the most important tribes – Vandals, Goths – were Arians. There was no western emperor after 476. At the end of the fifth century Theodoric, the Gothic king, entered Italy bearing Roman official titles, and set up a regime in Ravenna that controlled Rome and imperial Italy. Arian heretic as he was, he brought with him a complete Arian clergy, that had nothing to do with the Catholic clergy.

The conversion of the barbarians to Christianity was often initiated by the wholesale submission of whole tribes. But it did not sweep away pagan culture in a few moments, as we are reminded every year by the feasts of Christmas, the Winter Solstice celebration of the northerners for which the nativity of Christ is a cheeky Christian misnomer, and of the New Year, in Roman usage the great

Left: A detail from Trajan's Column showing the Emperor Trajan greeting barbarians.

pagan feast of the Lupercalia. In Rome the ancient fertility rites of Cornomania were still celebrated annually, in the presence of the pope, as late as the eleventh century. Such pagan customs could persist obstinately in the heart of Christianity, and at the periphery there was often an interim in which the new religion sat uncomfortably with or above the old.

The overlap of Christianity and paganism can be glimpsed in two of the great heroic poems of north-west Europe: the Anglo-Saxon Beowulf, first written down around 700, and the Irish epic of the warrior-king Sweeney, of which the modern Irish writer, Seamus Heaney, has made an English version (*Sweeney Astray*) that is in its own right a great poem. Sweeney threw the psalter of the priest, Ronan, into the lake and killed his clerk. He was punished by being turned into a sort of half-bird, made to live on berries and to flit from one part of Ireland to another for the rest of his life, in a grotesque parody of the life of a Christian ascetic. In Beowulf the clash between the religions is not direct: the Danish pagan lords suffering from the depredations of the monster, Grendel, are pitied for their heathen sacrifice, and the Christian King of Glory is given recognition by the poet and his hero at various points, but the Christian deity makes no visible impact on the story.

Above: Detail from the late fourteenth-century Grandes Chroniques de France showing St Remigius Bishop of Rheims anointing Clovis I, King of the Franks.

Clovis the Catholic

The conversion to Catholicism of the Frankish King Clovis (c. 465–511) had important consequences both in his own and in the other barbarian kingdoms, including those of southern Britain. Clovis' wife was a Burgundian Catholic, although Burgundy was largely Arian at that time. The king's conversion was almost certainly due to what would now be called *raison d'état*. Clovis found his way to the south-west blocked by the Arian Visigoths. Either he decided that a holy war against them would be more successful than any other, or he may have become genuinely convinced, in the course of a successful campaign against another tribe, that the Christian God would favour him in battle. At all events, 'like some new Constantine', in the last years of the fifth century or very early in the sixth, he and his whole army were baptized by the Catholic Bishop of Rheims.

Clovis was at that point exceptional among the barbarian princes in preferring Catholicism to Arianism. The Bishop of Rheims was unlikely to make difficulties about receiving him, in spite of Clovis' bloodstained past, and of the bloodstained future that might reasonably have been expected of him. Clovis' war against the Arians was well stage-managed. Like any Roman king consulting the oracles, he went to the shrine of St Martin at Tours, laden with appropriate gifts, to ask for a sign. An appropriately military quotation from the Psalms was found for him, and according to Gregory of Tours, a divinely summoned pillar of fire led him to the decisive, successful battle with the Visigoths near Poitiers. He had fought the first holy war of the western barbarians. His baptism had neither dampened his aggressive ardour, nor blunted his cunning.

Above: Detail from the Golden Legend of Jacopo da Voragine, illustrating St Patrick greeting a king, an indication of the rising influence of the Christian Church on secular matters.

Left: The story of Adam and Eve as illustrated in the ninth-century Moutier-Grandval Bible, in the Carolingian Abbey of St Martin, Tours.

Patrick and Columbanus

In Ireland, which had never formed part of the Roman Empire, the history of the conversions was different from elsewhere in north-west Europe. The faith was brought to Ireland by a fifth-century Briton called Patrick, who began a very gradual and piecemeal conversion of the tribes that was far from complete by the end of the century. Patrick also had effects upon the place of Latin and Greek in Irish culture. As a result of his mission and of the communities that he set up, Irish learning was lively and productive for some four or five centuries after him.

In 590, roughly a century after Patrick's death, a Northern Irish monk called Columbanus (543–615) came with his followers to north-eastern Francia. To Frankish monasticism, and later to the monasteries of northern Italy, Columbanus brought Irish learning and peculiarly Irish penitential practices, which allowed a much more individual approach to sin and penance. The earlier Western Christian approach to the erring had been that they should ask the Christian community for forgiveness. The tradition brought by Columbanus, which also had its parallels in the Eastern Christianity of the time, was that the troubled soul could discuss the sinner's plight with a holy person who was a sort of spiritual doctor but also a friend; from this discussion the appropriate penance and restoration could take place.

Monastic Rules

The sixth century was a critical time for the way men and women followed a dedicated and secluded coenobitic, or monastic, life in the monasteries and hermitages. Withdrawal from the world to live in the manner followed in the Egyptian desert, in cells located outside the ordinary commerce of the world, often in frighteningly inhospitable localities, was a pattern that needed an ordered society to back it up, and a certain level of general economic prosperity. For example, very large numbers of the Egyptian desert coenobites — up to several thousand at a time — would finance their charitable activities by offering themselves on the labour market in the harvest season. When social disorder prevailed, such things were more difficult, and the monks could themselves be a destabilizing influence, if they were not subject to proper controls.

There had been many attempts in East and West to stabilize monastic life around some simple and workable principles. The variety of this way of life was very great, as were the delicacy and complexity of the spiritual and collective issues. Particularly influential over a very long period were the anonymous 'Rule of the Master', and the 'Rule of Benedict of Nursia', both composed in central Italy in the first part of the sixth century. Both were drawn up for particular communities, and not as some sort of code of general application.

The distinguishing characteristic of the Rule of St Benedict is its assumption of a sheltered community of celibate males dedicated to a life of prayer, which to a large extent is to be prayer carried out in common. The spiritual aims are those of the community rather than those of the individual. Why this rule, which was intended for the governance of the communities headed by Benedict and none other, imposed itself over such an enormously wide area of the Western church, is almost certainly a consequence of the wisdom and moderation of the advice that Benedict gives for leadership. He is not prescribing for heroes of the spiritual life, nor for great mystics, but for honest people who want to give of their

Below: Seventh-century high cross and uncapped round tower at Clonmacnoise, County Offaly, Ireland. Monastic settlements arose in Ireland as monks integrated their secluded, devotional lifestyles into the surrounding communities, thus making their spiritual influence communal rather than individual.

© Ancient Art & Architecture Collection

Left: The ruins of St Catherine's monastery in the Sinai desert. In the sixth century, the template for monastic settlements was forged in inhospitable regions.

best in a calling that is quite certainly very difficult to describe. Anyone who has ever had anything to do with pastoral care will recognize the moral world of which he speaks, and would be prepared to value what he says about it.

Of the abbot the Rule says:

'The abbot should remember always what he is and what name [sc., father] he bears, and know that to whom more is committed, more is demanded. Let him realise also what a hard and difficult task he has undertaken, to rule souls and to adapt himself to many different characters. This one he must praise, that one rebuke, another persuade, and according to each one's character and understanding he must adapt himself in sympathy so that he may not only not suffer loss in the flock entrusted to him, but may rejoice in their increase. Above all things let him not give his principal care to fleeting earthly things and so neglect or undervalue the salvation of the souls committed to him... Let him study to be loved rather than feared. Let him not be impetuous or anxious, autocratic or obstinate, jealous or suspicious, for so he will never be at rest... and let him so temper all things that the strong may wish to follow, and the weak may not draw back.'

Left: A monk milking a goat from a sixth-century fresco in the Monastery of Saint Catherine, Mount Sinai. The coenobite monks could not survive in isolation without some interaction with society, such as offering themselves for work during the harvest.

St Benedict's work took place in dioceses of central Italy that were controlled or strongly influenced by the Roman Church, and this is reflected, as Dom David Knowles, a Cambridge professor who had lived under it, said[3], in the simple, strong outline of government prescribed in the Rule. The just use of authority, and submission to it, on the implied model of the Roman household, are the core of the Rule. Authority in the monastery had not merely to be present, but to be audible, visible, articulate. The aim was to serve and praise God in a common life separated from the world. The means to achieve this end were the liturgical life of common prayer, the private life of meditation, prayer and study and the domestic life of manual or artisan labour, in the house, the garden, or the workshop.

The social assumptions made in the Rule are widely different from those of Eastern or Irish monasticism. It presupposed a social organization that would be disposed to support the coenobite community through the gift of quite substantial estates; when it makes no reference, for example, to the harvesting of produce, it assumes that the monastery will be supplied by a late Roman large country estate or latifundium. The Rule sees the monk only in the house or in its immediate vicinity; it does not see him labouring in distant fields, or carting produce far from the home grange. Nor was the monk to be in the slightest degree a wandering holy man. He could not even become the spiritual friend and counsellor of the laity, save under the strictest of controls. St Benedict chose for his two most important monasteries sites that were hard of access: Subiaco in the valley of the Aniene southeast of Rome, and Monte Cassino, astride the main line of communications between Rome and Naples. Neither foundation was by any means in the desert.

The Rule was perfectly suited to a Western Roman world in which provincialism and regionalism prevailed everywhere, where the local landowners and the rulers above them were quite willing to subsidize coenobitic life by the gift of estates. In return, the monastery educated some of their male children, perhaps also taking others that were indisposed to, or unsuitable for, the military life, and retaining them in the community. They were also very willing to support nunneries (for whom the Benedictine Rule could be easily adopted) which would retain their surplus females. Beyond the transactions in children that were involved, there were questions of the honour that accrued to a family from supporting works of holiness that led to salvation, and of the holy men who remembered families and local principates in prayer.

The monasteries were not private schools filled with aristocrats. They took recruits from every walk of life, just as the coenobite communities had from the outset. But the role of the noble families in financing, building and endowing the monasteries was bound to be reflected in the way they were run. In a world where government authority was precarious at least, they were in a privileged position that was open to abuse, and the austere precepts of the Rule did not always protect them.

Gregory the Great

At the end of the sixth century, the monastic tendency and the clerical leadership of the upper nobility were well represented by Gregory (c. 540–604), the grandson of a former Roman bishop, but a great aristocrat who occupied the office of Prefect of Rome. This was some half a century after the armies of the eastern Emperor Justinian had carried out a precarious reoccupation of the Italian peninsula, the north of which had been swiftly lost again to the heretical Arian Lombards. Gregory founded a monastery on the Aventine hill, not far from the Roman Forum, but he was not at first its abbot. Gregory joined the Roman clergy reluctantly. He was a gifted and tireless writer, whose work

Above: A Benedictine monk painting a statue of the Virgin and Child. The detail comes from the Lambeth Apocalypse c. 1260.

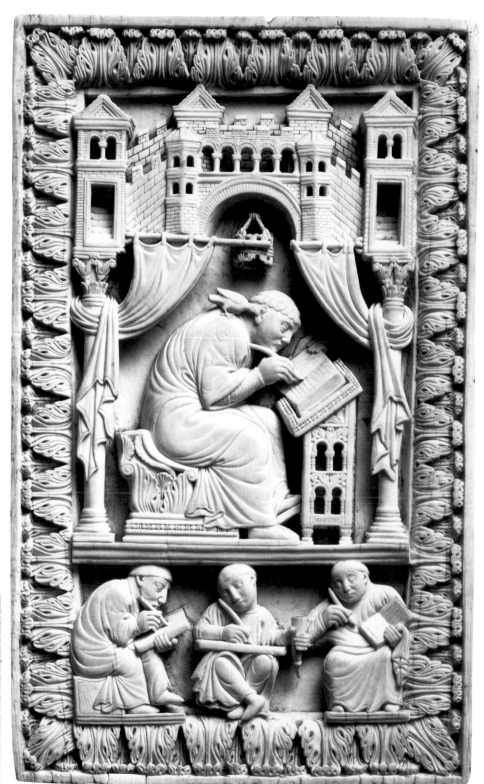

Above: A sixth-century mosaic showing Justinian I and his retinue. A learned man, Justinian was emperor of the East Roman Empire from 527 to 565.

Left: St Gregory writing with scribes below. Gregory was a gifted and tireless writer. His Pastoral Care became one of the great medieval handbooks.

103

Pastoral Care was to become one of the great handbooks of the Middle Ages. (Two centuries later, it was translated into English by King Alfred.) Even more reluctantly, in 590 he became Pope.

Gregory's career was a classic example of the way in which government often devolved upon the Church at this point of the early Middle Ages, because no one else was competent to assume it. The Roman Church was by his time the greatest landowner in western Europe, with lands located not only all over Italy and its islands, but in Gaul and as far to the east as Asia Minor. Its land management was modelled on that for the imperial domain. It had taken over the provisioning of the city of Rome, and had become something between a huge soup kitchen – that looked after thousands of refugees from barbarian incursion elsewhere – and a public ministry of supply. The imperial palaces and the ancient public buildings, lacking all maintenance, were literally falling down; the aqueducts and walls (the walls measured some 20 km/12 miles) were now looked after by the Church. It fell to Gregory to negotiate with the Lombard armies who were pressing down upon the 'Roman' (or Byzantine) lands from the north.

Above: A silver penny minted during the reign of the Anglo-Saxon King Ethelbert of Kent.

Right: A reliquary surmounted by the head of Oswald the Holy, King of Northumbria. The crown is made of gold, enamel, and decorated with precious stones and pearls.

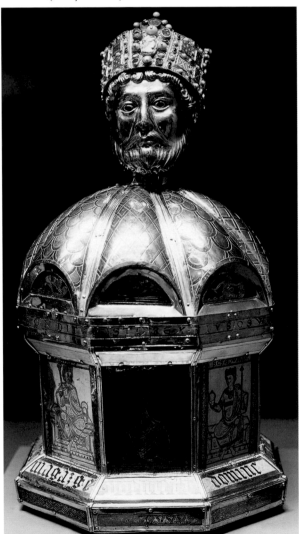

From Gregory's Rome, an advance missionary venture set out in 596 for England; the second, effective missionary party left two years later. It was headed by the monk, Augustine, who brought Roman monasticism to England at the same time as Christianity. His mission was not initially addressed to the Anglo-Saxons. The invitation to send Roman priests had come from Ethelbert, the King of Kent, the formerly Jutish south-eastern province of England. Ethelbert had a Frankish, Catholic wife. Gregory had jumped at the chance of bypassing the usual missionary ventures that departed from the Catholic periphery; instead he despatched evangelists direct from Rome, which he regarded, in an entirely excusable way, as the centre.

Gregory was a subject of the Byzantine Emperor; south of Rome lay the solidly Byzantine provinces ruled from Naples, and north-east was located the real Byzantine seat of government in Italy, that of the Exarch in Ravenna. Gregory had recently protested the Patriarch of Constantinople's assumption of the title of 'universal patriarch'. But in the barbarian north-west of Europe, the eastern Emperor's writ did not run.

The English mission occupies a special place in the development of medieval papalism, because no other ecclesiastical province among the barbarians came to have the same dependent relation on the Roman see. The missionary leader, Augustine, after a short period received the Kentish king as a Christian, and baptized also large numbers of his subjects. King Ethelbert was said to have understood that Christianity must be freely accepted, and so the mass baptisms were perhaps not so indiscriminate as some of those that took place on the Continent. But the king was still said to have favoured those who converted more than those who did not, which was not without effect on his nobles. After his consecration as bishop, Augustine sent back to his principal in Rome for guidance on a number of topics. The correspondence at once made Gregory into a lawgiver for the bishops in Britain.

The English conversion, like the Frankish conversion, depended on the evolution of barbarian princely politics. For reasons that are hard to penetrate, the most powerful king in the island, who exercised some sort of hegemony over the rest, Edwin, King of the Northumbrians, decided to take a Kentish wife and subsequently to accept Christianity. The second decision was only taken after much hesitation. Edwin adhered to it, and so, after some disputes over the succession, did his successor Oswald. The eventual conversion of the Anglo-Saxons was thus assured. Oswald finally imposed Catholicism on his own dominions, and made its eventual victory only a matter of time in the areas south of the Humber. The victory that established Oswald's position was achieved not over the pagan Mercians (who were converted at a later point after being defeated by Oswald's son Oswy), but over the British King Cadwalla.

The Roman mission of Augustine to Britain imposed a Roman pattern of Catholicism upon the country, which might under different circumstances have accepted Christianity from the Celtic

Above: St Cuthbert shown both praying in the sea and having his feet licked dry by sea otters. A monk looks on. The image comes from Bede's Life and Miracles of St Cuthbert.

Left: The ruins of Whitby Abbey, Yorkshire. The original abbey was founded in the seventh century and was the site of the Synod of Whitby called in 663.

church, which had already converted most of Scotland by the time the Roman missionaries reached Northumbria, and that had quite a body of adherents in the south of the country. The triumph of Roman Catholicism in Northumbria was not automatic, because Oswald, the key figure in the conversion of the North and the Midlands, had already made contact with the Celtic monks among the southern Picts, and been converted by the Celtic monks of Iona, before he came to power there. Scottish, Celtic-trained bishops were called to fill sees in the Northumbrian church.

Right: An illuminated manuscript – the Codex Amiatinus – which was produced in Jarrow, Northumberland. It shows Christ in majesty with angels and the four Evangelists.

© Bridgeman Art Library, London

The Synod of Whitby

But a reckoning between Roman and Celtic traditions in Britain came with sharp disputes about the mode of tonsuring clerics, which differed between Celtic and Roman practices, and about the system for fixing dates for the annual celebration of Easter. The Synod of Whitby, held in 664 under the presidency of the Northumbrian king to decide the matter, ended in the victory of the Roman observance. The Celtic monastic tradition continued to influence strongly the Northumbrian church, particularly through St Cuthbert, at a time when the Celtic influence of Columbanus was very much alive on the Continent in the Frankish church. But the essential discipline of the English church continued to be Roman, more so than was the case in Francia.

Especially because of the way in which they had combined Roman and Celtic monastic and cultural traditions, the Northumbrian monks at Jarrow were among the most vigorous and flourishing monastic communities in western Europe by the early seventh century The Venerable Bede (c. 673–735) was at this time a towering figure, the most cultivated monastic historian of his time, a master of the difficult science of chronology, and the biographer of the far-off contemporary Roman popes.

The art of the illustrated book was practised there and in Ireland in a manner to make their manuscripts the envy of Europe.

By the early seventh century, the barbarians who had settled in the western Empire and its former possessions were virtually all Christian. Some had secured their position in the Empire as Arian Christians but they, with the rest, had virtually all become Catholic. Franks, Anglo-Saxons, Visigoths, Burgundians, Ostrogoths, even the Lombards, who had been the especially violent enemies of the Catholic 'Romans' in central Italy, had all accepted the Catholic traditions. Only in Anglo-Saxon England was there an organic historic root in the faith that had actually been sent to them from Rome. On the lower Rhine, there were still substantial pockets of paganism, such as that of the Frisians, and in many other areas outside the old Roman frontiers, such as the territories of the Saxons, the still huge areas of the pagan German hinterland remained. In much of southern Italy and Sicily, in Rome, and in the enclave of Ravenna in eastern Italy, the Byzantine emperor remained in rather precarious control. But the more or less assimilated barbarian tribes of the western Empire, although no longer subject to any real form of temporal control by a Roman emperor, were in one sense culturally Roman through their Catholic belief, and through the Latin culture of the clerical class.

Patronage and Privilege

In their conviction of the conquest of death through holiness, and the accessibility of the martyred and saintly dead to the living through the frequentation of their tombs and the veneration of their relics, late Antique Christians had introduced a new form of sociability. Social privilege was not indifferent in the pursuit of the holy. Networks of influential families undertook to uncover and conserve holy relics, and to move them to new locations where the patronage systems could influence the bishops to have them displayed in the way the patrons wanted. Under popes such as Damasus, the Roman catacombs became great museums to illustrate holiness and martyrdom. In Rome, the great shrines such as those of St Peter, St Paul, St Lawrence, and the churches dedicated to the other martyr-popes, became places to lodge petitions with these influential denizens of eternity. In Christendom the healing of the sick, which paganism had assigned to innumerable divine shrines, was transferred as a duty to the shrines of the Christian holy ones. A shrine such as that of St Martin of Tours benefited from a long series of miracles, and became one of the great shrines of north-west Europe.

A process of extending the patronage networks of the powerful to the halls of eternity took place in the monasteries of the barbarian kingdoms. Not only did the princely barbarian families place their own members in the monasteries they founded and provided with huge landed endowments, but their kinsfolk in the monasteries also set up for them a most elaborate system of commemorating family members for ever in the prayers of the monks. Books of remembrance were produced, specifying who was to be remembered in the liturgy and on which days. These books became a sort of Almanac de Gotha that recorded all the appropriate members of the princely families who had endowed the foundations.

The universal charitable aims of the churches were by no means forgotten in this rush to commemorate the rich and powerful. Both in the eastern and western Empire, and within its western successor-states, the redistribution of wealth to the poor and destitute was one of the main functions of the bishops and the monasteries. Dealing with the huge influxes of refugees that occurred in the disturbances of the barbarian invasions was the duty of the Church; no other authority even attempted

Above: Detail of ceremonial sceptre surmounted by a bronze stag, from the seventh-century Sutton Hoo Treasure.

107

to cope with it. The penetration of the holy into most aspects of life continued, as it had in pagan antiquity. But in Christianity the holy men had assumed new functions that allowed their ideas of the holy to penetrate the social fabric of noble barbarian society. Later in the Middle Ages the Church was to take upon itself many of the former functions of the state. A few of these transfers have been astonishingly long-lived. Despite the religious upheavals of modern times, the bureaucracy of the late Roman Empire continues today to pursue a shadowy existence in the bureaucracy of the Roman Church.

1. Mons.L. Duchesne, *Early History of the Christian Church*, trs. C. Jenkins, vol.3 (London, 1924), p.226.

2. Quoted by Peter Brown, *Augustine of Hippo: a biography* (London, 1967), p. 287.

3. *The Monastic Order in England* (Cambridge, 1941), p.9. The quotation from the Rule of St Benedict is from D. Knowles, *Christian Monasticism* (London, 1969), pp.34–35.

Left: Tenth-century German book illustration. At the top St Boniface meets his martyrdom at the swords of the Frisians.

7

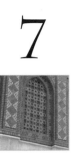

CHRISTIANITY AND THE RISE OF ISLAM

In the early seventh century Christianity continued to inhabit the space and the time of the Roman Empire, its domicile since its beginnings. Here and there it had slipped outside the Roman frontiers, as it had done in Ireland at one end of the Roman world, in Armenia at the other. In India it had made a tentative minority appearance, in Persia and Mesopotamia a more tenacious one, one of whose manifestations – Christian Nestorianism – had penetrated as far as China. In Arabia it had reached some areas in the west of the peninsula, although Judaism was probably better known there. But although there were a few great Christian centres that lay outside the territories of the Roman Empire at its fullest extent, Christianity continued to be firmly based in the lands of the old Empire, which contained all the bishoprics of its apostolic and heroic periods, from Alexandria and Carthage in North Africa to Jerusalem, Antioch and Rome.

At the beginning of the seventh century it started to become apparent just how precarious was the hold of Byzantium on its south-eastern lands. The Sassanian Persian armies had secured the upper hand in Mesopotamia and Armenia during the last part of the sixth century, and had had to be bought off. In 607 the Persians started to overrun Syria, and in 614 they occupied Palestine – where they carried out great massacres, and seized the relic of the true cross from Jerusalem – and subsequently Egypt. It looked as though Christian rule in a huge area might be finished.

Left: The Dome of the Rock (built 688–91) in Jerusalem.

Above: Stone inscribed with Chinese and Syriac characters from Singanfu in China. In the seventh century, Singanfu was the site of a flourishing Christian church.

Above: A detail from Piero della Francesca's The Legend of the True Cross. In 629, Emperor Heraclius forced the Persians to return the relic of the true cross. He himself walked up the Via Dolorosa carrying the relic.

There was a Byzantine reaction under the Emperor Heraclius (575–641) that looked for a time to have succeeded. In 622 he launched a daring strategy that aimed to recover the lost provinces by a direct major attack on the Iranian part of the Sassanian Empire. In executing this plan he showed the utmost coolness, keeping his main army in the field even when the Avar tribes from the Danube besieged Constantinople in 626. The defence of the capital was conducted by the Patriarch and the Emperor's son with desperate gallantry, and its success was attributed to the intercession of the Virgin. It was on this occasion that the Patriarch Sergius composed the great Acathistos hymn to the God-bearer, the mother of Christ. Heraclius engaged the main Sassanian army in 628 in the mountains near the ruins of Nineveh, and destroyed it. The Persians were compelled in the following year to return the lost provinces, the Christian prisoners, and the relic of the cross.

In the Christian western Empire, no one took orders from the Emperor in Constantinople any more, outside the strongpoints of Byzantine Italy. One of those strongpoints was Rome, which was the only bishopric in the west to have apostolic origins. When it began in apostolic times, the language of the Roman Church had been Greek, and in the early seventh century Greek was still the official language used by the imperial government in Rome, although Latin had become the language of the western church. The Roman pope was still a bishop inside the political life of the eastern Empire, although the relations of the western with the eastern church and its Emperors were often poor: in 653 Pope Martin was arrested for treason, flogged, and sent to die in exile in the Crimea.

The western church thus remained in contact with the east through its Roman leadership, and the western barbarian kingdoms remained in trading and other relations with the eastern Empire. However,

Above: Persian illustration from Reasons for Charity by Mustafa al-Shukri showing the mosques at Medina and Mecca, the centre of the Islamic world.

Right: Page from a handwritten version of the Qur'an, possibly eighth century. The fragment is from the Great Mosque in San'a, Yemen.

© AKG London

these things took place against the background of a deterioration of almost all the late Roman towns in the west, and very sharp declines in population and production, with consequent changes in settlement patterns, that far preceded the seventh century. The prolongation of the Christian space of the ancient Roman Empire into that of the barbarian kingdoms was in that century to be cut by the irruption of a new political order into the Near East and the southern Mediterranean.

Muhammad, the Messenger of God

The new Islamic order was to place new barriers between Christendom and its historic origins. The bishoprics of the barbarian West had for a very long time been drifting apart from the ancient patriarchates of the East. But Islamic supremacy in the East meant, in spite of their common Christian roots, that they ceased finally to share a common cultural world. In one sense the barrier has never been completely lifted, even in periods like those of the early crusades, or the times of modern Anglo-French hegemony in the Near East and North Africa. In another sense, however, the Mediterranean Sea was never totally closed either to the West or to the East: in spite of pirates, holy warriors and war fleets, there remained a certain porosity that for centuries allowed merchant ventures to leak from one culture to another, whether Islamic, Byzantine, or Latin.

In the early seventh century a member of a pagan merchant family in Mecca in the region of the west-Arabian Hijaz began to have intimations, as though from behind a veil (Qur'an, 53.1-8; 2.97-98), from divine spiritual beings, that he ought to carry out certain actions, and to say certain things to those around him. The Hijaz was the economic and cultural centre of Arabia, linked by commercial ties with Syria and Palestine, and so a main point tied indirectly with the Mediterranean. Christian monks and Jewish rabbis walked the roads of Arabia, and their doctrines were far from unknown in Hijaz.

The subject of the visitations, Muhammad (570–632), thought of himself as God's messenger.[1] In the Qur'an (42.51) he is reported to have said that 'it is not fitting for any human being that God should speak to him except by revelation or from behind a veil, or by sending a messenger to reveal by his permission what he will.' Some of the suggestions that reached him from on high were connected with the revelations he knew to have been made in the past to earlier prophets. He was thus guided to follow the religion of Abraham, the breaker of idols and the worshipper of Allah, although this did not mean that he was to follow the Jewish religion as understood by some of the tribes in the Hijaz. From the beginning the spoken word seems to have figured as a sort of future scripture. In one of Muhammad's earliest revelations, in which he was told to 'recite', a part of the revelation is of what the Lord 'taught men by the pen'. The verb for 'recite' can also mean 'to read' (Qur'an, 96.1-5).

The history of the text of the Qur'an is as obscure as that of the Christian Gospels. After Muhammad (whose literacy is still disputed) went to Medina he is known to have employed secretaries, and tradition records his having dictated a particular passage (sura) to a scribe. But the writing down of the revelations was only partial, and at the time of the prophet's death large numbers of the revelations were 'in the hearts of men', known only through their having been memorized by his companions. The first written collections are thought to date from the time of the caliph 'Uthman, probably between 650 and 656. But at this stage knowledge of the Qur'an was still based on memory more than on writing: the emergence of something pointing towards a canonical text did not begin for another half-century.

Mecca was the city of many important gods as well as a trading centre, and Muhammad's messages were received by most of the merchant rulers, including some members of his own tribe, with derision. He was described as a teller of old wives' tales. The close relation of his revelations both to Judaism and to Christianity would have come as no surprise to his hearers, since some tribes within the mercantile orbit of Mecca had been converted to one or another of the two faiths. His assertion of a single god, Allah, and his denunciation of the polytheists, or worshippers of many gods (who came for him to include the Christians, whom he defined as Trinitarian) were commercially and politically inconvenient, because they threatened the benefits that Mecca obtained from being the resort of many polytheist traders and worshippers.

By 622 the position of Muhammad in Mecca had become untenable, because his kinsfolk had become unwilling to protect him further against his enemies. His adherents helped him in his flight (*hijra*) to the oasis of Yathrib (that later became Medina, the town of the prophet, or messenger), some 200 miles distant, and took an oath of support. The community that joined him in submission to his divine messages became the nucleus of a political and religious organization. Submission to the will of Allah that had been intimated by Allah to his messenger was the core of the new religion.

Above: Points of pilgrimage at Mecca and Medina, from a sixteenth-century manuscript by Futuh al-Haramain. Muhammad was born in Mecca but by 622, his position there had become untenable and he was forced to flee to Medina, the 'city of the prophet'. His flight is known as the hijra.

Above: Mural painting in the Imam Zahdah Chah Zaid Mosque, Isfahan, Iran, showing martyrs of the Shi'ite faith fallen in war.

The 'submitters' were called Muslims, and the community of Muslims was called (from the same root, *salima*) Islam (Qur'an, 3.19, the true religion with Allah is submission [Islam]).

Muhammad received many divine messages at Medina. Their complexity and often very practical nature have frequently given the impression that he was fundamentally a lawgiver who set up a written code of behaviour. But this is to do a grave injustice to a man who came to announce and warn, and to convey a moral message that was just as much directed to the heart as had been the teachings of Jesus. Muhammad told people that they must face God's judgement for their works on earth, on a last day when all created things will be rocked by earthquake, and men and women will be sentenced to heaven or hell for their behaviour in this life, receiving credit for their acts of kindness and mercy, and perdition for their misdeeds.

The believers who seceded with Muhammad formed what can in modern terms be described as a political society, that lived, fought and prayed together. It was in a sense tribal, although beyond tribes. His position was without parallel in the Arabian society of his time. He called his supporters the party of God (*hizbullah*): it was their duty to struggle in the way of God (the verb is *jahada*, hence the noun, holy struggle, *jihad*) with all those who scoffed at, derided or impeded God's messenger. This opposition to Muhammad and his cause was deemed *fitna* (persecution), referring to acts of disintegration or dissolution of the community; the implication is political in this case as well as religious. Muhammad said that slaughter is an evil thing, but that fitna is worse, implying quite clearly that sacred war was the duty of the community when such sacrilege was otherwise unavoidable. To struggle in the way of God preserved, however, its primary general meaning of spiritual and moral effort. The armed struggle was only a single aspect of this general moral struggle. For an individual Muslim, jihad can include all acts of worship, and other acts associated with belief.

However wars of secession from the Meccan community were duly fought, and they formed a pattern that served to define a part of the duties of the believer. When they ended with his victorious return to Mecca in 630 of the Christian era, Muhammad had become an Arab sovereign as well as a divine messenger. Those who from the start had been his faithful helpers (*ansar*) enjoyed a specially privileged position in the regime. That there were others whose position had at one time or another been ambiguous, or who had become hostile to him, is obvious from the names he attached to classes of followers described as 'hypocrite' or 'hesitant'. The families of Meccan notables who had opposed him down to the very last moment, nevertheless became the great, rich princes of the Arab Empire that formed after Muhammad's death.

His troops crossed the Byzantine frontiers in 631, and were bloodily repulsed. The following year he himself led a great military expedition to northern Hijaz and as far as the Syrian-Byzantine border at Tabuk. The campaign of Tabuk ended without any major engagement; Muhammad marched back to the Hijaz, and in 632 made his last pilgrimage to Mecca. The sermon he gave on this occasion represents his last thoughts on what is called in the modern West the expansion of Islam. He gave four months' grace to those non-Muslims who were not protected by previous treaties. At the end of this period of grace the unbelievers were to be slain wherever the Muslims could find them (Qur'an, 9.29). Quite whom among the unbelievers Muhammad had in mind when he gave this sermon is uncertain: there were at that time still many unconverted tribes among the desert Arabs, of whom we know that Muhammad entertained a very poor opinion. But he may, equally, have been thinking of the 'Roman' (i.e. Byzantine) Christians, or even of the Sassanian Persians. Shortly after the 'farewell' pilgrimage, Muhammad died in 632 at the age of 62.

By the time of his death Muhammad had come to be a divinely inspired model of human conduct for many thousands of men and women. His courtesy, kindness and patience, his moderation in every aspect of behaviour, including food and drink, his ability to combine firm leadership, including leadership in war, with generous and charitable actions, produced a style of life that ordinary people could reasonably hope to imitate, and that his followers managed to transmit to succeeding generations by recording their memories of him. He had rejected cruel and destructive things such as infanticide and blood feud, although he had not managed to impose his way of life upon the wider Meccan community without armed combat. His leadership had shown remarkable political adroitness. He had avoided the ascetic excesses of many holy men, but he still brought to the world glimpses of his experience of things that to him and subsequently to others seemed to have transcended the merely human.

When Muhammad is compared with the other great prophet of the same ancient world, the contrast with Jesus is not as sharp as Christians have made it in the past. A dissimilarity has traditionally been seen between a celibate Jesus and a Muhammad whose uxorious disposition was allowed to dominate the society he made and the paradise he promised. The contrast is false: Muhammad regulated the law of marriage in a way that was undoubtedly reformist and humane, and no less rigorist than the comparable views of Jesus. His use of sexual imagery in religious contexts is considerably more restrained than what is to be found in the Song of Songs.

The other traditional Christian reproach, that Christianity is a religion of love and Islam a religion of power, points to great differences in the lives and teachings of the two prophets, but when put in this stark way is really no more than ancient holy-war propaganda. The teachings of both Muhammad and Jesus place the love and mercy of God at the front of the models of life that they propose. Because as Muhammad saw it he could not carry out the divine commands that were transmitted to him without resort to arms, the resort to arms was incorporated in the society that he founded, although only as a last resort against moral impiety (fitna). In Christian terms the result was as though the Emperor Domitian had adopted Christianity at the end

© Imam Zahdah Chah Zaid Mosque, Isfahan/Index/Bridgeman Art Library, London

Above: Seventeenth-century mural painting from the Imam Zahdah Chah Zaid Mosque, Isfahan, Iran, depicting the fourth caliph of Islam, Ali-ibn-abi-Talib (602-661), murdered on his way to the mosque at al-Khufah.

Right: An illustration from the Persian Makamat (Literary Gatherings), a collection of rhyming adventure stories by Abu Mohammed al Kasim ibn Ali (1054–1122). It shows the Caliph's guard.

of the first Christian century, instead of the Emperor Constantine having done so in the fourth. The society inspired by Jesus was unarmed for almost three centuries, and subsequently armed. The society inspired by Muhammad was armed almost from the beginning. There is a distinction, but it is perhaps finer than many Christians would like to think.

Muhammad had promised the believers in his last sermon that Islam as a religion would prevail over all other religions, that their enemies would be destroyed, and that they would (like Moses) be masters and God's deputies in the land (Qur'an, 9.33; 7.129). This was the political vocabulary of expansionism, but it would have remained a dead letter if the natural tendency of the Arab tribes to scatter in confused blood feuds had broken the quite frail basis of the Islamic community. That this did not occur after his death was owed to the religious piety, and also to the political and military ability of the small group of Islamic leaders (by no means all of them early 'companions' of the prophet), who chose to accept one of their number, Abu Bakr, the father of Muhammad's favoured wife, 'A'isha, as caliph or successor of the messenger of God.

The Caliphs and the Rise of Empire

The caliph made no claim to be the chosen recipient of further divine revelations, nor did those who came after him. He was in one sense no more than the prayer leader of the Muslims. But in effect the political leadership and the ultimate military command devolved upon him. The first task of the new caliph, without whose accomplishment there could have been no Islamic Empire, was to force the Arabian tribes that were scattering as was the natural tendency after the death of the big leader, to return to the discipline of Islam. In modern times this might be called a war against counter-revolutionaries, but it was understood in religious terms as a war against apostasy (the wars of the ridda).

Once victory in the wars of the ridda had given back to the Islamic community its obedient armies of religion, they could follow the injunction in the farewell sermon of Muhammad that the Muslims are brothers one to another, and are forbidden civil strife, and that they should fight all men who associate others with Allah in his divinity. The political results came practically as fast as the armies could move. Islamic holy war was in a very short time taken out of Arabia, first to Syria-Palestine, then Iraq, to Byzantine Egypt, and then to what remained of the Sassanian Persian Empire. No doubt, the armies of the caliphs of the second and subsequent waves of conquest were largely composed of non-Arabs.

How far the wars of conquest were genuinely wars of religion is hard to determine. A distinguished scholar, Bernard Lewis, observed that the army commanders were not particularly religious men, and that the truly converted and the pietists played little part in the creation of the Arab Empire. On the other hand, 'Umar (caliph during a critical period of the conquests, from 634–44) was clearly not indifferent to the military struggles. He made a special journey from Arabia to receive the submission of Jerusalem (see below), and he is also said to have incited the Muslim Arab armies to unite with those of a doubtfully Islamic Bedouin chief to attack the Persians in Iraq.

The consequences for the eastern Roman Empire were disastrous both politically and economically. The earlier victories of the Emperor Heraclius over the Persians were revealed as empty; all they had done was to weaken the Sassanian Empire so that the Muslims could conquer it. Egypt had been the granary of the Empire, and the maritime base for a large part of its sea power: both disappeared overnight. The territories controlled by the eastern Empire were halved. Both Alexandria and Jerusalem,

Below: The lavishly decorated interior of the Dome of the Rock. The Dome of the Rock was built on the site of Solomon's Temple in Jerusalem.

© AKG London

two of the historic deposits of the Christian faith and of its central theological traditions, became the local centres of a Christian religion that was still important in the eastern territories and which still had numerous adherents there, but that was now subject to political Islamic control, while its adherents had to pay the poll tax that was exacted from subject Christians and Jews.

The differences that Muhammad had had with both Christianity and Judaism had been profound. And since the core of his revelation was its independence of other revelations and its superiority over them, or at all events over the way their adherents had understood them, he often tended to lump them together as hostile, hypocritical elements. He told Muslims to 'take neither Jews nor Christians for your helpers' (Qur'an, 5.57). The followers of both religions had, he felt, sinned in a way that he felt to be more hurtful to him than any other: they had mocked and ridiculed him. So he told believers that they were not to allow Christians or Jews to turn them back to unbelief 'from envy'.

To Muhammad the Christians, but even more so the Jews, were not distant, unseen people whose religious texts he had read, or had had read to him, but people who played a part in the normal course of his life and of the lives of those to whom he preached. With the Jews he had had a working alliance for the first part of his stay in Medina, and they had impinged upon a central part of his religious practice in the first mosques. The first arrangement of the believers at prayer in the mosque had been to turn in the direction of Jerusalem to pray. Then, after a couple of years, Muhammad experienced a revelation that impelled him to change the direction in which his people turned to pray to that of Mecca, and also to abandon the observance of the Jewish Day of Atonement in favour of the fast of the month of Ramadan.

Neither of these changes was made without considerable hesitation, and it is probable that they were connected with political changes in his alliances in Medina. But, as had occurred some five and a half centuries earlier in Christianity, the results had been to remove any tendency the new religion might have experienced to become a Judaizing sect, and to open its path towards a new, universal mission. However, the first Islamic connection with Judaism had been profound, and it has been noted by a modern historian that, while the polemic of Muhammad in his lifetime with Christianity as recorded in the Qur'an was rather fragmentary and inconsistent, that with Judaism was coherent and intense.[2]

Muhammad's approach to Jesus was deeply positive, his approach to Christianity much less so. He made Jesus himself, although a miracle-worker, deny his own divinity (Qur'an, 5.116). He said of Jesus: 'It does not benefit Allah to take unto himself a son.' (Qur'an, 19.35). On the other hand, Jesus was to Muhammad the prophet and messenger of God, as he himself was to become. The purity and holiness of Mary were fully recognized by Muhammad. But the death of Jesus was treated very differently by Muhammad than by orthodox Christians. In the Qur'an Jesus is said to have been neither slain nor crucified; but Allah 'raised him to himself' (Qur'an, 4.157–158). The same goes for the first generation of Islamic religious tradition after the Prophet's death.

Christians in a Muslim Context

The position of the Christians and Jews in the huge areas newly conquered by the armies of Islam was a particular one. As 'people of the Book', understood as the Bible, they were not treated as pagans. Socially, also, it has to be remembered that the Muslims settled outside Arabia in the new Empire were nothing like so numerous as to constitute a majority, even if the first generation of Muslim converts is taken into account. Christians and Jews were not on that account over-privileged. They had to pay a poll tax (*jizya*) that Muslims did not pay and they could not marry Muslim women. In the later stages of the Islamic Empires they were subject to other restrictions that concerned their churches and synagogues, their dress, and other matters. But in the first stage of the conquests they still lived peacefully alongside the Muslims. There was no instant conversion of whole populations to Islam in Egypt or Syria, if only because people could only become Muslims by the acceptance of the Arabic language, sometimes also by a fictitious incorporation as clients of an Arab tribe. For quite a long time the situation in the newly Islamic lands resembled in some respects that in the West, where a foreign barbarian elite of a comparable but different religion cohabited with an anciently Christian population. But the ideological claims of Islam were too powerful to allow this to persist indefinitely.

The Muslims made huge borrowings from Byzantine culture, as may be seen by anyone who enters the Dome of the Rock in Jerusalem, with its rich mosaic splendours. Jerusalem occupied a special place in the sacred geography of Muhammad, because of its connection with the prophet Abraham. In later Muslim tradition, but probably not yet at the time of the construction of the first

O you People of the Book, overstep not bounds in your religion, and of God speak only the truth. The Messiah, Jesus Son of Mary, is only an apostle of God, and his Word which he conveyed unto Mary, and a Spirit proceeding from him. Believe therefore in God and his apostles and say not Three. It will be better for you. God is only one God. Far be it from his glory that he should have a son.
(Translation of inscription in the Dome of the Rock)

Right: A decorative female figure from the frescoes of the Palace of Qusayr Amrah, which illustrated the 'Umayyad Caliphs amongst the World Family of Kings.

Muslim sanctuary, the Temple platform was said to have been the arrival point of the miraculous 'night journey' of Muhammad from Mecca to the 'further mosque' (al masjid al-aqsa, Qur'an, 17.1). The second Islamic Caliph, 'Umar, made a special journey to receive the submission of Jerusalem after its fall to Muslim forces, within only seven or eight years of the Prophet's death in 632. 'Umar would not pray with the Christian patriarch of Jerusalem in his church, although invited to do so, because such an act would have sanctified the place to Muslims, and so made it inaccessible to Christians. Instead, he went to the platform of the Temple Mount to pray, where the Dome of the Rock and the al-Aqsa mosque were subsequently built within the Muslim holy area. The Qur'anic inscriptions that were at the end of the seventh century placed round the inside of the Dome of the Rock, assert the oneness of God. They also ask for a divine blessing upon Muhammad and equally upon Jesus, emphasizing the position of Jesus in Islam as prophet and messenger. In this city sacred to both religions, the anti-Christian polemic of the Qur'an is still present in the inscriptions, but muted.

By the early eighth century the Islamic Empire extended from Visigothic Spain and Morocco in the west to the Indus valley in the south-east and to Transoxiana in the north-east: North Africa including Egypt, Syria-Palestine, Iraq, the whole Persian Empire had been swallowed up. In the 'Umayyad desert palace of Qusayr Amrah there was placed in the caliphal baths a fresco that was intended (against several Islamic precepts) to represent the 'Umayyad caliphs as part of the world family of kings. The eastern Emperor, the last Visigothic ruler of Spain before the Muslim conquest, the Negus of Ethiopia, the Sassanian Emperor of Iran (who had been displaced permanently by the 'Umayyads) and, probably, the Chinese Emperor were all illustrated.

The caliphate, which remained united until 750, had become one of the great civilizations, and had entered into a close relationship with the cultures of both Hellenism and Iran. But towards the end of that period the aims and nature of the caliphate suffered a further change. The close emulation of the Byzantine Empire that had marked many of the policies of the earlier 'Umayyad caliphs was practically abandoned after the failure of the last great medieval Islamic siege of Constantinople in 718. The brief Islamic flirtation with political Hellenism had ended.

The period between the first and the last siege of Constantinople by the Arabs, between 673 and 717, was a time of great peril for eastern Christianity. It is true that the internal dissension in Islam imposed a form of peace for a long time after the lifting of the first Muslim siege in 677. The great quarrel with Islam had results on the internal religious quarrels about the divine and human natures of Christ that had been splitting the Byzantine Empire for over a century, and that had contributed to rendering imperial rule precarious when the Muslim attack came in Palestine-Syria and Egypt. In 681 the areas of the Empire that had most strongly supported the doctrine of a single divine will in Christ, 'the one incarnate nature of the Word', had passed under Muslim control, and their bishops were no longer in a political position to influence imperial policy.

Rome and Constantinople Reconciled

At the Council of Constantinople in 680-1 the doctrine about the divine nature of Christ that had been expressed at the Council of Chalcedon in 451, was reasserted in a manner on the whole acceptable to the Roman see, whose legates were chosen to preside, after the Emperor, over the conciliar sittings in the imperial palace. The doctrine of two natural wills and two energies co-existing in Christ, that was unacceptable in Alexandria and Jerusalem, was reasserted. The Emperor's

attempt to satisfy the Roman see was manifest; the conciliar decisions quoted both the 'tome' or written opinions on the matter of Pope Leo I (pope from 440–61), and the opinions of the choleric Athanasius, who in his life had never found much favour in the imperial court.

The papal legates at Constantinople were satisfied. The doctrines that were now proclaimed, under authority of the Council and the eastern Emperor, were the same as those whose profession only a generation earlier had caused Pope Martin to be driven by imperial persecution and exile to his death in the Crimea. On the other hand, the Emperor preserved his imperial dignity in 681 by insisting on the condemnation of Pope Honorius (pope from 625–38) for heretical views on the same matter. The topic of Honorius was still found to be embarrassing to the strong papalist cause when it was raised in opposition to the thesis of papal infallibility, during the sittings of the Vatican Council in 1870.

The entente between Rome and Constantinople lasted only a very few years. In 692 the Emperor Constantine IV held a council in Constantinople (the 'Quinisext') that issued disciplinary provisions for the clergy entirely unacceptable in Rome. When the Emperor instructed the imperial official in Rome, Zacharias, to arrest Pope Sergius and to dispatch him for trial in Constantinople as Pope Martin had been dispatched in 653, the regional troops mutinied, and Zacharias had to escape their wrath by hiding under the papal bed. The order of arrest was never executed.

Behind the theology of the Council of Constantinople in 681 the clash of Muslim arms can be heard in the background. In Italy the pressure of the Lombards had been severe for over a century. Significantly, in the same year that the Council of Constantinople was called to conciliate the bishops in the western part of the Empire, a peace was signed by the Empire with the Lombard barbarian intruders, which recognized most of the conquests in northern and central Italy that they had made at Byzantine expense during the preceding century. The huge pressures that were operating

Above: The Little Palace of 'Amrah, in Jordan, which was built during the reign of Caliph Walid I (705–15).

Above: The Third Council of Constantinople, which was held in 680–81 under Pope Agatho and Emperor Constantine. The image is an engraving taken from a fresco in the Vatican.

on the Empire everywhere from the borders of Syria and the Euphrates to the garrisons remaining in North Africa, meant that the frontiers in Italy – which included Rome, now only fifty or so miles from the nearest Lombard forces – were increasingly going to be left to their own devices. The story was already familiar from the experiences in the north-west of the Roman Empire in the fifth and sixth centuries. Like those experiences, it was going to have consequences for the Christian religion in the West.

1 Albert Hourani, *A History of the Arab Peoples* (London, 1991)

2 J. Wansbrough, *The Sectarian Milieu: Content and Composition of Islamic Salvation History* (Oxford, 1978), pp. 40-1

Left: Constantinople under siege. The city was besieged many times and was taken on different occasions by both Christians and Muslims. In 1453, Constantinople finally fell to the Muslims.

8

THE BOOK
AND THE SWORD

At the beginning of the eighth century, Constantinople was still one of the wonders of the world, and still the centre of a large, powerful, militarily active Empire. It had remained the great Christian, Roman capital that Constantine had intended when he inaugurated the city in AD 330. Although the urban population had much declined after the first Arab assaults, until they began, it had been the greatest and most populous city west of the Chinese Empire. During the 40-year rule of Emperor Justinian (527–65) it had been the centre of the biggest and most concerted military and administrative effort made by the Roman Empire since the third century, and had sent armies to recover lost provinces in Italy, in Sicily, in Dalmatia, in Africa, in Spain. The armies were smaller than the old armies, but still very effective.

Above: Map of Constantinople dating from 1422. Haghia Sophia is visible.

The huge churches and imperial palaces of the capital had been marvelled at since Constantine, but Justinian added new wonders, most notably the great church of the Holy Wisdom (Haghia Sophia) that he had constructed after the destruction wrought by the Nike riots in 532. Building activity was not confined by Justinian to the east. Much of his construction in the west was military, but some, as in Ravenna, was of splendid churches and palaces. Byzantine culture, which had become more and more ecclesiastical in nature, nevertheless retained its basis in late Greek language, literature and philosophy.

Left: Haghia Sophia, Constantinople. It was originally built as a church but has been a mosque since 1453.

© AKG London

Above: Mosaic from the south vestibule of Haghia Sophia. The Virgin Mary and Child are enthroned between Emperors Justinian and Constantine.

Below: A Saracen is converted to Christianity by the power of the image of the Virgin Mary. The detail comes from a thirteenth-century French manuscript.

© Bibliotheque Nationale, Paris, France/Bridgeman Art Library, London

Justinian lived too long; the great plagues, and the Persian military revival that started to take place before his death, announced the numerous cracks in a logistically overstretched and (in both senses) overtaxed system. But the apparatus of taxation that was the big engine of the military power and central organization of the state, and that had long since vanished in the barbarian west, remained in being long after Justinian. Politics remained essentially court politics, as they had been since Augustus.

The Arab invasions, and the consequent removal from the Byzantine world of Syria-Palestine, Egypt and what had been left elsewhere in Africa, profoundly disrupted an economic and military system that had been in place since the beginning of the Roman Empire. The last Arab siege of Constantinople in 717–18 had put the entire existence and ideology of the eastern Empire in question. Although the siege was lifted, and the chanting of the great hymn to the Virgin on the city walls appeared to have been heard on high, the culture had experienced a trauma from which it was not to recover easily. Not unsurprisingly, a culture so profoundly religious in character exhibited its shock in a religious form.

Leo the Iconoclast

At this critical moment, leadership was seized in 716 by Emperor Leo III, the 'Isaurian', whose dynasty took its name from their tribal home in the Cilician Taurus mountains, in south-west Asia Minor. Leo adopted a radical religious tendency that objected strongly to the veneration of the images of the incarnate saviour and of other saintly persons, beginning with the Virgin Mary. For at least three centuries these objections had been swamped by the almost universal devotion accorded to such images, to which the faithful sometimes attributed quasi-magical powers of healing and intercession. Some religious images were credited as having been 'not made with hands'. In a religion that was by now so imbued by the sacramental principle which endowed the physical symbol with holy qualities, this was perhaps almost inevitable. But in a culture that had a long tradition of rational theology, as well as one of sentimental devotion, there was bound to be a reaction. There was certainly some scriptural basis for objection to religious images, not only in the Old Testament (Exod. 20: 4), but in the New Testament (Acts 17:29). The whole question was to resurface powerfully in Protestantism during the sixteenth century.

Until this time the only audible objectors in the eastern church to the cult of images had been small dissenting groups such as the Paulicians, who had originated in the Upper Euphrates area, and who refused the veneration of Mary as well as that of images. But Leo III, perhaps feeling his way towards a radical religious view that would unite and energize the Empire (as Constantine had done in the fourth century), decided to turn the whole Church within the Empire towards an 'iconoclast' or image-breaking policy: venerated images were to be condemned and avoided, perhaps destroyed, following an edict issued in 726. Perhaps Leo was also somewhat influenced by his resentment of the scant military input of the great tax-exempt religious persons and bodies at a time of military emergency.

Leo III's iconoclasm gained wide popular support in the eastern areas of the Empire, particularly among the Armenians, but not in the western; it was particularly abhorred in Rome, which continued formally to be a part of the eastern Empire. Leo III was also criticized in the east as being 'Saracen-minded', since Muslim objections to visual representations of the human form were well known.

There were no specific prohibitions of images (as opposed to altars or idols) in the Qur'an, but the Muslim fear of depicting anything that might remotely be understood as associating something or someone else with Allah in his divinity had led to an avoidance of them.

Left: St Nicephorus the Patriarch and the Holy Father looking on while iconoclasts break images.

There was no doubt about the military effectiveness of Leo III and his immediate successors. Faced by the prospect of extinction, the Empire pulled itself together and recovered much of its military muscle. There was a military reorganization of the army, based on big military regional divisions known as themes. The constant pressure from Muslim armies in Asia Minor was resisted much more successfully than before, for this reason and also because the trend to withdraw first-line troops to the capital had been reduced with the final breaking of the siege in 718. Asia Minor was not, of course, the only battle front. The Bulgarians were emerging as a formidable pagan fighting force south of the Danube, a danger to important grain-growing areas. The Slavs had begun their capillary penetration southwards into the Balkans.

Slowly, the military crisis of the Empire ended. The Islamic caliphate split for the first time in 750, and the far western lands in Iberia (Andalus) went their own way under 'Umayyad leadership, while the usurping 'Abbasid caliphs transferred the seat of power to the new capital of Baghdad. The centre of Islam was no longer in Syria, so close to the Byzantine border, but in Iraq. There were still big Muslim fleets, especially in Alexandria, but they were no longer subject to immediate control by caliphs. As they began to reform their armies with Turkish slave troops, 'Abbasid military concentrations became based in distant Khurasan and Transoxiana.

The war of the frontiers was not over, and to some extent it was a permanent holy war on both sides, conducted on the Muslim side by the mujahidin, on the Christian side by frontier levies called akritai. But the great conflicts of main armies became very infrequent, and big naval engagements ceased. The eastern imperial court remained rich and powerful, able to dazzle western barbarians with its pompous ceremony, on which much of the 'Abbasid caliphate court's ritual state protocol was to be based. But the economic power and heavy population of the old Byzantium had been sapped. Byzantine revenues were dwarfed by those of the caliphate, and the most flourishing and opulent urban life was henceforth to be found in the great Muslim cities.

In the western part of the Byzantine Empire the results of the setbacks of the seventh and early eighth centuries made themselves felt in a falling away from former imperial loyalties, which had repercussions all over the western barbarian world. The process began in the 720s with tax strikes in the Italian provinces in protest against the iconoclast measures of Leo III. The leaders of the resistance were the Roman popes. They got full support from the central Italian provincials, who had received no effective imperial protection against Lombard oppression.

In Francia the late Merovingian kings, feeble descendants of Clovis, had been unable to exert full royal power, and had been superseded in its exercise by the so-called mayors of the palace, of the noble line of the Arnulfings. Five years earlier, in 749, the Arnulfing Pippin III, 'the Short', had sent an envoy to Pope Stephen's predecessor, Zacharias, to discover 'whether it was good or not' that the infant Merovingian King of the Franks, on whose behalf he purported to rule, did not exercise royal power. In a classic statement of *Realpolitik*, Pope Zacharias had replied that it was better that he who had real power should be king, rather than he who did not. The result had been an assembly of the Frankish magnates at Soissons, which hailed Pippin as king, and saw him anointed with holy oil (a Biblical procedure entirely unfamiliar in either barbarian or Roman political life), probably by the Anglo-Saxon Bishop Boniface, who had first visited Rome in 719, and was in effect a papal agent. It was a momentous political intervention by the Roman popes in the affairs of a Frankish church and nation with which papal contact had until that time been polite rather than close.

The Popes and the Franks

In 753, when the main iconoclast council was held in Constantinople, Pope Stephen II made a revolutionary diplomatic move that had the effect of shifting the main political ties of the Roman bishop from the legal ruler of the Roman Empire to a Frankish nobleman who held effective but only doubtfully legal royal power in the Frankish kingdom. Pope Stephen took advantage of the presence of a special Byzantine envoy in Italy to accompany him on a mission to the hostile Lombard King Aistulf, in the Lombard capital, Pavia, in northern Italy. When the conference broke up without result, instead of returning with the imperial representative to Byzantine territory, Pope Stephen set off alone from Pavia to Francia.

Having made this unheard-of papal journey, Stephen was welcomed at the beginning of 754 by King Pippin at Ponthion in Champagne. He had come, in effect, to claim the political reward due to the pope and to the formerly Byzantine population of central Italy, for the support given by his predecessor Zacharias to Pippin's crowning and anointing as Frankish king. The pope fell before the king in sackcloth, and asked, with ashes on his head, if he would support the suit of 'St Peter and of the republic of the Romans' for the restoration of their rights in Italy by the Lombards. The promise was made, and formally ratified the following spring in the presence of the Frankish magnates. Pope Stephen had been asking for a Frankish invasion of Italy, and he obtained two Frankish military interventions, in 755 and 756, which damped down Lombard aggression, and which also foreshadowed the establishment of what in modern times came to be called the papal state. More important than that, he had established a link between the Roman bishops and the Frankish kings that was to have momentous consequences for Christian Europe.

The Frankish kingdom had, by the mid-eighth century, become the most powerful of all the

Below: In the eighth century the Roman papacy forged strong links with the Frankish kings.

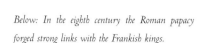

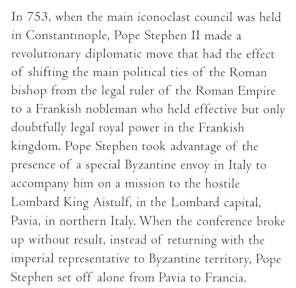

barbarian realms. When Pippin III died in 768 it stretched from the Pyrenees and the Mediterranean coast in the south, to the lower Rhineland and Frisia on the Atlantic coast in the north. On the east it included Thuringia and reached as far as the borders of Bavaria; to the south-east it included most of present-day Switzerland west of the Allgäu and the Brenner. When Pippin's son Charles became undisputed king of this huge conglomeration of tribal groups in 771, he had the military means to become the most important barbarian leader since Theodoric the Ostrogoth, at the turn of the fifth and sixth centuries. He was at a later period known as Charles the Great, or Charlemagne. Unlike Theodoric, if Charlemagne chose to intervene in the Roman province, he had the additional advantage that he was no Arian heretic, but ruler of a nation that had been Catholic for over a century and a half, and that had been linked with Rome by Charles's father, who had established a close treaty connection with the Roman bishop.

The Frankish kings had already been, earlier in the eighth century, the sponsors of a huge work of Christian evangelization on their eastern and northern borders, in Frisia and Saxony. It had mostly been carried out by Irish and Anglo-Saxon missionaries, to whom it had seemed natural to obtain papal as well as Frankish patronage. Those clerics, of whom Boniface was the most important as an intermediary, were sometimes to die as martyrs, but they had established a position at the Frankish court that played its part in setting up the Roman-Frankish alliance.

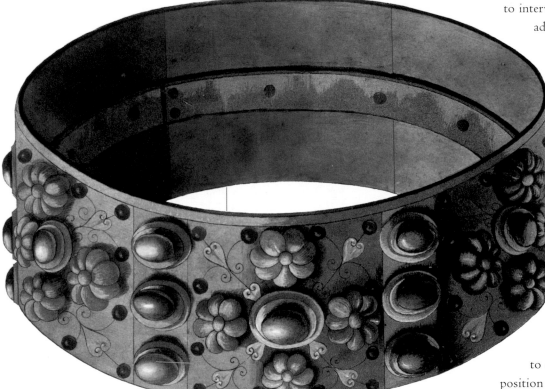

Above: The Iron Crown of Lombardy with which Charlemagne was crowned King of Lombardy in 774. Much later, in 1805, Napoleon insisted on the same crown for his coronation.

Charlemagne and Military Expansion

A man of immense energy and ambition, Charlemagne seems to have had an extraordinary awareness about the huge geographical and cultural realms in which he was able to move. Though illiterate until late in life, he attached great value to learning, and somehow seized fiercely on the huge possibilities for power that lay in the imposition of clerical social discipline in a centralized way. To most modern men and women who live in Charlemagne's old lands or their neighbours, the church liturgy probably looks like an optional extra in the religious life; to an eighth-century person, it could appear to be a way to regulate the lives of hundreds of thousands of people who had no other binding union but a vague allegiance to a distant tribal superior.

To Charlemagne it seemed that hegemony, the aim of all barbarian kings, had to be accompanied by religious conformity that was sponsored by the hegemonial monarch. When he started the huge

ARENTVRETTANAMETINTERRELIQVA

Left: A side panel from an altar showing the adoration of the Magi. It was commissioned by Ratchis, Duke of Spoleto. It is a fine example of Carolingian art.

wars on his northern and eastern borders, which lasted almost until his death in 814, his aim was conversion, and forcible conversion if necessary. While he was never going to change the tribal nature of barbarian society, he realized that the nearest thing to imposing what we would call assimilation upon conquered or recently subject areas, was a form of Christianity that was subject to some sort of

Right: Carpet page preceding St Mark's Gospel with circles of interlacing design linked with angular interlacing, from the Book of Durrow (c. 650–700). The art and literature of Christian Ireland would not be unknown to a man of Charlemagne's cultural stature.

Above: Charlemagne and his army fighting the Saracens in Spain in 778.

central control. For this reason the great wars on the eastern borders across the Rhine with the Saxons, that were fought for 33 years 'with immense hatred on both sides', and accompanied by transportations of populations and atrocious group punishments imposed on the Saxons at various times, ended in mass baptisms. After 785, evasion of baptism was to be punished by death. This

policy did not meet with the entire approval of the
missionaries working in Germany, and Charlemagne
later modified it.

Early in the reign, in 773, Charlemagne marched
into northern Italy and finally suppressed the old
Lombard kingdom, of which he later assumed formal
kingship. In the following year he went south, arrived
in Rome on Easter Saturday, 774, and proceeded to
guarantee to Pope Hadrian the control of the main
areas of so-called Roman settlement in central Italy,
probably according to the peace treaties the Lombard
kings had made with the Byzantines at the end of the
previous century. In effect, north Italy, with some of
the south-lying Lombard dependencies, had been
annexed by the Frankish king, and the rest of central
Italy, including Rome and the former Byzantine
exarchate of Ravenna, made into a Frankish
protectorate under the Roman bishop. South Italy
continued to be a part of the Byzantine Empire,
which was powerless to affect these proceedings.

The territorial alliance with the Roman see was
only a part of Charles's designs. These aimed at
making the Roman see into the pivot of far-reaching
ecclesiastical and even cultural policies, which would
have further political results. The onset of the new
Frankish order was due to the political misfortunes of
Hadrian's successor as pope, Leo III, who was a
Roman cleric of no great family, unlike his aristocratic
predecessor. Four years after his election in 795 some
Roman nobles rebelled, accused Leo of serious
misdemeanours, and tried to have him blinded without
trial. He was lucky enough to escape, and to travel into
Saxony to find Charlemagne, whom he had earlier greeted
as 'the new Constantine', and to ask him for assistance.

Pope Leo was sent back to Rome with a
Frankish escort, honourably, but in fact to await some
kind of legal procedure that would clear his name. His
labouring under such a severe political disadvantage
meant that he was unlikely to reject any procedure named by the Frankish king that would have the
effect of releasing him from suspicion. Charlemagne himself came to Rome at the end of 800 with
the intention of settling the matter. What occurred in 800 has continued to have effects on the
political and cultural shape of Europe into our own times.

*Above: Image of the Byzantine Empress
Irene, a fervent anti-iconoclast. The mosaic
is in the Haghia Sophia.*

© AKG, London

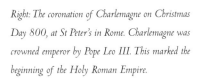

Right: The coronation of Charlemagne on Christmas Day 800, at St Peter's in Rome. Charlemagne was crowned emperor by Pope Leo III. This marked the beginning of the Holy Roman Empire.

© Musée Goya, Castres/Giraudon/Bridgeman Art Library, London

The Origins of the Holy Roman Empire

Two days before Christmas, before a council of bishops, the pope was allowed to clear himself from the charges made against him, by the procedure of declaring his innocence under oath, one that had some precedent in papal history, and also happened to be a standard barbarian legal procedure. On Christmas Day 800 Charles went to mass in St Peter's dressed not as a Frank, but in the official Roman costume (the Greek *chlamys*) of a Roman patrician, a high office which had been bestowed on him by a previous pope. At the end of prayer Pope Leo placed a crown on Charles's head, and the Romans in the basilica acclaimed him as emperor. The ceremonial acclamatory hymns proper to the greeting of the (previously Greek) emperor in Rome were sung, and Pope Leo ceremonially prostrated himself in the Greek fashion.

As far as the Byzantine government was concerned, this was a meaningless, illegal pantomime. Unfortunately for that government, not only was it without military or practical power to intervene in Italy, but it was itself experiencing an awkward interregnum. The problem had grown from a series of intrigues that had to do with the opposition to iconoclasm of Irene, the former empress of Leo IV (who had died in 780). Having been regent during the minority of her son Constantine VI, Irene carried out a coup against him after he had assumed personal rule in 790; in 797 she had had her son blinded and imprisoned, and herself resumed the government. It became arguable that, as a woman was legally incapable of ruling it, in 800 the Roman Empire was vacant; it was an argument unlikely to convince anyone in the East.

Charlemagne's assumption of the imperial title had been canvassed in court circles for some time before 800, and can probably be seen quite as much as a result of barbarian ideas about recognizing hegemonial kingship, as an acceptance of concepts that genuinely sprang from late Roman tradition. Charles certainly had not needed the imperial title to execute his church policies so far as they touched the Roman bishops, who continued to be, as they had been before, the chief and most honoured bishops of the Frankish realm, worthy to receive gifts appropriate to their status. But the assumption of 'empire' was to have consequences that Charlemagne almost certainly did not anticipate, particularly for the protocol that later had to be followed for a Frankish – or other western – king who wanted to assume the title.

For what can from 800 onwards be called without qualification the Western Latin Church, the reign of Charlemagne had absolutely decisive results. The split from iconoclasm was no longer the only reason for the distance at which the western bishops held themselves from the eastern. In 787 Irene had succeeded in holding an eastern church council against iconoclasm in Nicaea, which had been attended by two papal legates from Rome, who assented to its proceedings. Charlemagne had himself entered some cavils against Nicaea, or rather, his theologians had done so for him, and he held his own western church council that looked at the matter, in Frankfurt in 794. From the eighth century onwards, and particularly from the imperial coronation of 800, the real differences between the Western and Eastern churches centred on their contrasting allegiances to different political masters. The independence of the Roman see from the Frankish ruler, or of the dynasties that followed the Franks, had subsequently to be worked out in centuries of tortuous and often painful political and religious experience.

Charlemagne's religious, educational and cultural policies were achieved partly through the elitist means of the influence and leadership provided by the small group of clerics attached to the court,

Above: Gold sword and scabbard, set with precious stones, said to belong to Charlemagne.

Right: An illuminated manuscript from Kaernten, Austria, from the eighth or ninth century. It shows Charlemagne and his wife.

© AKG London/Erich Lessing

and also through the insertion of many requirements regarding religious matters into the general instructions ('capitularies') that were circulated throughout the various areas of the Frankish realms by the imperial envoys ('missi'). The new monasteries that were being established, especially in the newly-annexed areas, became the centres that received, protected and diffused this new court-inspired religious culture. In this respect the new Frankish nobility, preferred by the ruler, and granted huge lands and offices everywhere in the new Empire, became an integral part of the official religious culture by their endowment and patronage of the new monastic centres.

Literacy and Liturgy

Charlemagne insisted that the court bishops and literary and clerical figures around them collected and to some extent distributed Christian and also pagan texts that not only reached a high standard of calligraphy and book production, but of grammatical and textual competence. Even the laymen around the court were encouraged and, up to a point required, to reach a good standard of literacy. In a sense the regime attained its cultural aims through the holy books, whether of the Scriptures themselves, or of the liturgy, or of theology. 'Carolingian minuscule' script has exerted an influence that reaches as far as the modern printed book. The court literati also created new kinds of court panegyric of the ruler, comparable in type to those of the post-Constantinian period, although always written in Latin and not in Greek. And some of them had to be capable of sustained theological argument, up to a level that would bear some comparison with the theologians of the contemporary Eastern church.

Probably the most influential and formative of all Charlemagne's church measures was the insistence on a degree of general conformity of the liturgies that were to be followed in the churches. There were areas where local and ancient church custom had to prevail, as in the proud dioceses of Milan and Ravenna, and in some dioceses of Francia, but in the rest of Francia and in the newly converted areas the Roman Rite, known as the Gregorian Sacramentary, was followed everywhere.

There is a contrast between the enormous geographical and political extent of Charlemagne's Empire, and the relatively modest size of the cadres that he employed to govern and serve it. The contrast exists, too, in the modesty of the physical proportions of much of what he built. His conquests

Below: Charlemagne was very keen to foster education throughout his realm. This is an early ninth-century illustration of The Fountain of Life from the Court School of Charlemagne.

lenr fut fait sj ordona lempere de be
mr en vne ville q ano restie p passa
uller loyre p puis en frace pour passer
le fort yuer. Tout ainsi le fist. Ja soit
ce q ce fust moigs honnestemt p moigs
honourablemt quil ne couenoit Comt
loyr lemperr deuat sa mort departit
lempire en trops pties aux trops enfas

E dyable noustre mortel e
nemy h ason pouoir est toq

Right: Charlemagne divided his kingdom between his three sons, Pepin, Charles and Louis in 806. After his death, his Empire disintegrated.

of Saxony and Bavaria, his pushes beyond the Elbe into lands of Slav tribes such as the Wilzi, his subjection of many of the Danes, his thrusts into what became the Frankish county of Barcelona, added up to give him a degree of control over a great part of western Europe. But in spite of this, in comparison with the old empires his tax base was tiny, and his military control spasmodic. Charlemagne's palace at Aachen was not huge, nor was its church. Nonetheless, Charlemagne's imprint still lies heavily upon the mentalities of the churches of Europe, and influences the ways in which they define themselves relative to the Eastern Christian and the Muslim worlds.

Below: The throne of Charlemagne in his chapel at Aachen.

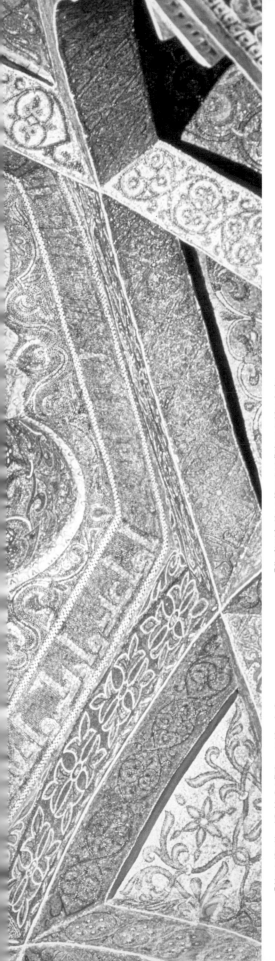

9

EAST AND WEST

The last half of the eighth century was the period of the maximum flowering of early Muslim urban life and culture. The Muslim world had become a huge market for goods and human resources (including slaves) that stretched from the North African cities to central Asia and the Indus, and through the Indian Ocean to south-west India. The eastern Caliphs, having built a splendid new capital at Baghdad, presided over a genuine successor-state to the old empires of the Iranian Sassanians and the Hellenistic and east Roman rulers of the Near East and North Africa. The caliphal armies were at this point centrally controlled and tax-financed through the central diwan, and in this respect were probably nearer the late Roman imperial troops than were the Byzantine ones of the same period.

Above: Medallion of the Caliph of Baghdad.

Islamic buildings drew on a range of historical reference that was just as widely based as Islam itself.[1] The basilica (in its non-ecclesiastical, Roman urban form), the Christian church, the Iranian palaces, the ziggurat, the Zoroastrian temples, all left their mark. The pattern of late Roman urban design in the Near East was enormously important for Islam, although a lot of the public spaces of the Hellenistic town were rejected, and filled by rather haphazard Muslim inner-urban sprawl. The needs of the mosque were very simple: they could be met by almost any large enclosed space that would accommodate the adult male population for Friday prayer. Such spaces could be large enough to hold an army, as in Samarra, Cairo (Fustat), or Qairawan. The liturgical needs were simple: a recessed niche (mihrab) to indicate the direction of prayer was the minimum. Neither the minaret nor the pulpit-like minbar, which was usually of wood, was essential.

Left: Interior of the dome over the mihrab — a recessed niche indicating direction of prayer — in the Great Mosque in Cordoba, Spain.

Right: View of the city of Cairo with the Fustat mosque in the foreground.

Right: A ninth-century astrolabe from Iraq. Islamic science flourished at a time when European culture was at a nadir.

Greek culture, or at any event the Greek culture of philosophy, mathematics, and medicine, was assimilated by a new Arabic-speaking intelligentsia, or in some areas by an Arabic and Persian-speaking intelligentsia. There was, for a time, some attempt to conciliate Muslim theological ideas with Greek philosophical concepts, which was a sort of parallel to the great theological debates in Christendom. It was, however, a relatively short-lived debate in the Muslim world, which ended in the victory of the fideistic thinker, Al-Ghazali (1058–1111), and the subsequent rejection of the Greek philosophical forms as a normal language for theology. The severely scriptural basis of Islam triumphed easily over abstract speculation, especially after the development of a clerical class that had acquired a big body of traditional religious learning. If there was a Muslim religious world that could speak to the Christian religious experience, it was probably to be found in the mystical discourse of the Sufis. Yet there was also a world (overlapping with Sufism) of the popular appreciation of holy men and holy objects, in which Christians and Muslims venerated the same local saints and relics without much distinction.

Christianity within Islam did not die. By the end of the third century after Muhammad, the society of the Islamic zone had become for something like a majority Islamic society. For the first time the majority of the population would contrast the *dar al-Islam*, the peaceful house of the Muslims, with

© AKG London

Left: The Council of Abelda in Toledo, Moorish Spain. It was held to establish a peaceful means of incorporating Christian religion into a totally Muslim culture.

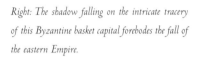

Right: The shadow falling on the intricate tracery of this Byzantine basket capital forebodes the fall of the eastern Empire.

the *dar al-harb*, the house of war of the infidel. Not that this meant the persistence of endless great wars with all the Christian powers; on the contrary, even if war was endemic on the frontiers, the more usual relationship between Muslim and Christian powers was one of truce.

The Christian sects within Islam were, at least, no longer troubled by persecuting Christian governments. The Armenians, whose kingdom was for a long time subject to the 'Abbasids, although on occasion it escaped; the majority Egyptian Christians ('Copts'); the Syrian or Jacobite church; the so-called Nestorians (whose sphere of influence stretched to China) were all groups that had objected to the definitions of Christ's nature made by the Council of Chalcedon. They are all groups whose religious affiliation has survived into our own times.

So long as the caliphate was controlled, outside Andalus, by a single caliphal succession, Byzantium could hope for nothing better than to hang on. In 782 an 'Abbasid force reached the Bosphorus and exacted tribute from the Empress-regent, Irene. In 806 the Caliph Haroun al-Rashid himself led a big army that crossed the Cilician Taurus to take the main city of Cappadocia, Tyana (Kalesihisar) and marched on into the Anatolian heartland to ravage Ancyra (Ankara). Muslim sea power returned in great strength in both the eastern and western Mediterranean: Crete fell in 825, and two years later a great force embarked from Tunis under a Persian mujahid leader, and got a toehold in Sicily (still Byzantine at this point), which led to the eventual Muslim occupation of the island.

Fortunately for Byzantium, the 'Abbasid caliphate was undermined, something like a century after its foundation in 750, by centrifugal forces that were both religious and regional. The last great caliphal expedition marched in 838 through western Anatolia to take Amorium in Phrygia, on the western edge of the Lycaonian highlands, where it captured an entire Byzantine army. But this turned out to be the last great Muslim success in Anatolia before the Seljuk conquests of the eleventh century.

Above: A Christian and Muslim play a game of chess, symbolizing the wary truce between the two religions.

Caliphs in Control

The most fundamental of the splits in Islam had occurred only a generation after the death of the Prophet, in 656–61. The legitimacy of the election of the fourth Caliph, 'Ali, the cousin of Muhammad and the husband of the Prophet's daughter, Fatima, had been challenged unsuccessfully by a coalition that included the Prophet's former most favoured wife, 'A'isha. Subsequently a second opposition movement headed by the discontented 'Umayyad governor, Mu'awiya, again challenged 'Ali's right to rule. Mu'awiya outwitted 'Ali, so that when the latter died in 661, his right to the caliphal title was still in some doubt. The second round of the dispute between Mu'awiya, proclaimed Caliph after the death of 'Ali, and 'Ali's family, was fought in 680, when 'Ali's son Husayn contested Mu'awiya's right to the caliphal title, and was killed by an 'Umayyad army at Karbala, in Iraq. The 'Umayyad dynasty was henceforth unchallenged until 750, but from Husayn's death sprang the religious party of the adherents of 'Ali (shi 'at 'Ali or Shi'as), which has remained in Islam until the present day, and was the moving force behind the Iranian revolution of the Ayatollah Khomeini in 1979.

In the ninth century, the 'Abbasid dynasty was challenged on two levels, the dynastic and the religious. In Iran, in Khurasan, in Egypt, and in Tunisia, it found itself in the second half of the century displaced from effective power by local dynasties or rebellious governors whom it could not dislodge. Other dissident movements surfaced. By far the most important was that of the Shi'a, who initially organized successful movements in Arabia and North Africa (the Maghrib), and then, in 969, eventually put into place in Egypt an anti-'Abassid caliphate of 'Fatimids' (i.e. supposed descendants of 'Ali and of the Prophet's daughter, Fatima). But throughout the ninth century there had also been lesser dissident movements of various sorts, which all contributed to weaken the caliphate of Baghdad. There had been a half-century in which the caliphs emigrated to Samarra, near the ethnically Turkish centres of their military recruitment programmes, but their return to Baghdad in 892 had not re-established their power.

Byzantium Fights Back

This Muslim disunity enabled a strong Byzantine comeback during the ninth century. The Byzantines had recovered sufficiently to survive a strong attack on Constantinople by the Russians of Kiev in 860, to make the Anatolian

Above: Muslim soldiers recruiting for the armies of the faithful.

Below: This foundation stone carries an inscription in ornamental Kufic script. It mentions the construction of the grand palace of Monastir in 966 and the exodus from Magrib to Cairo on the order of the Fatimid Caliph al-Mu'izz, King of Egypt from 969.

Left: A Coptic funerary stela. The Copts were an Egyptian Christian sect who survived within an Islamic context.

153

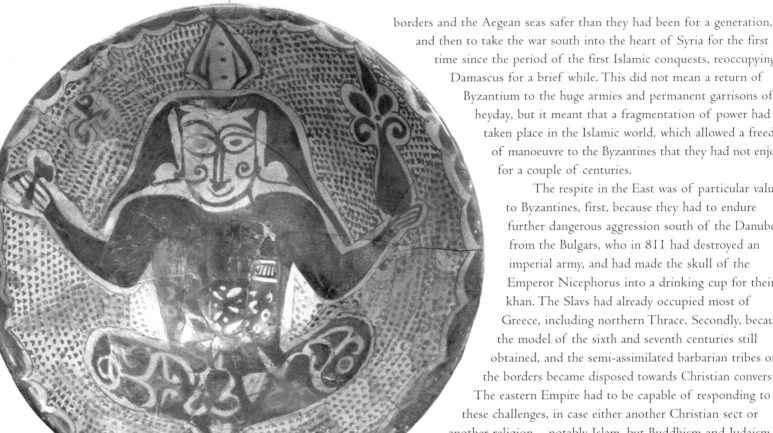

borders and the Aegean seas safer than they had been for a generation, and then to take the war south into the heart of Syria for the first time since the period of the first Islamic conquests, reoccupying Damascus for a brief while. This did not mean a return of Byzantium to the huge armies and permanent garrisons of its heyday, but it meant that a fragmentation of power had taken place in the Islamic world, which allowed a freedom of manoeuvre to the Byzantines that they had not enjoyed for a couple of centuries.

The respite in the East was of particular value to Byzantines, first, because they had to endure further dangerous aggression south of the Danube from the Bulgars, who in 811 had destroyed an imperial army, and had made the skull of the Emperor Nicephorus into a drinking cup for their khan. The Slavs had already occupied most of Greece, including northern Thrace. Secondly, because the model of the sixth and seventh centuries still obtained, and the semi-assimilated barbarian tribes on the borders became disposed towards Christian conversion. The eastern Empire had to be capable of responding to these challenges, in case either another Christian sect or another religion – notably Islam, but Buddhism and Judaism were other competitors – was received by the pagan barbarians before Orthodox Christianity.

The Danish Angle: Alfred and Cnut

Above: A lustre bowl from the 'Abassid period. The image of Buddha indicates the extent to which Islamic pilgrims travelled.

Right: The Alfred Jewel. Alfred defeated Guthrum at the battle of Edington (878) and converted the Dane to Christianity.

All over the Christian borders, the situation was approximately the same. Islam remained a powerful, aggressive counter-culture that still possessed the capacity (although, perhaps, no longer the will) to win the religious and political battle with both the East and the West of Christianity. But in the fragmented world of the frontier tribes, the more military and cultural advances the outer tribes made, the more they became inner tribes, disposed to receive the religion of their hosts. An English pattern is provided by the reception and baptism of the victorious Danish King, Guthrum, by his Anglo-Saxon opponent, King Alfred, at Wedmore. Within a century and a half of that baptism, Cnut, the grandson of the Danish king, Harald Gormsson, who had converted to Christianity in 960 or thereabouts, became not only the Danish but also the English king. Cnut was a pious Catholic ruler. He made a pilgrimage to Rome, but also built a palace at Winchester whose iconography celebrated the pagan origins of the dynasty.

Left: Cnut and his first wife, Aelfgifu, at the Palace of Winchester. A pious Christian, Cnut became King of England in 1016.

In the West, the Frankish Empire half a century after Charlemagne's death in 814 split into a western, a 'middle' and an eastern kingdom. In the same period the Christian West had been subjected to severe external pressures, everywhere from Iberia and the western Mediterranean to the North Sea, the Channel, the Danube and even the Rhine. The Arab maritime attacks on Italy and the islands of the western Mediterranean were part of a pattern that stretched from Crete to Bari and Barcelona.

Christianity under Siege

An especially disastrous attack for the Roman bishopric that was now one of the two or three chief centres of the Frankish Empire took place in 846, when an Arab army from Aghlabid Tunis landed at Ostia, brushed aside the defence forces of Anglo-Saxon pilgrim troops, and sacked Rome on the north bank of the Tiber. The two great apostolic shrines of St Paul and St Peter, both full of piously donated treasures, were plundered, and the tombs of the apostles wantonly smashed. In the next few years St Benedict's monasteries at Subiaco and Monte Cassino were also sacked. Modern archaeology has found the Muslim hammer marks on the old Petrine memorial stones under St Peter's, and has found the prostrate doors of the great southern monastery of San Vincenzo al Volturno, lying where

Above: An Arab trading ship. The skills of seamanship perfected in more peaceful times meant that Arabian sea power posed a particular threat to Christians in the Mediterranean.

Right: King Sven Forkbeard, father of Cnut, drowns in 1014. He had led the Northmen on various successful raids along the eastern English coast.

they were thrown by the Muslim despoilers of the same years. Big Muslim 'pirate' bases appeared at Bari (that became for a time a Muslim emirate), and at the mouths of the Rhone and of the Tyrrhenian Garigliano.

Islam was only one of the areas – although the largest – from which attacks on the Christian kingdoms were launched. The sea power of the Scandinavian and Danish tribes, or Northmen, enabled them to raid a huge area, which stretched from the north of Ireland over much of the English coastline and interior, to the Rhine estuary and to the area of north-west Francia, later named Normandy after them. They also raided south as far as the southern Rhineland. The Hungarians raided the entire course of the middle and upper Danube, until they virtually met the limits of Northmen depredation on the Rhine. All over Europe the population retreated to defensible 'castle' or 'burgh' sites. Although the Frankish Empire had come into being through huge, occasionally mobilized armies, it did not possess the kind of taxation and type of central administrative basis that had allowed the late Roman and the subsequent Byzantine Empires to keep armies in being that were large and effective enough to defend enormous lengths of frontier. The 'Marches' that the Franks created on their borders were not militarily strong enough to support this degree of pressure.

The Avars, a Turcic people, had been contained in Pannonia between the Drava and the Danube by the last great military effort of Charlemagne. Behind them to the east and the north were the Slavic peoples of various branches, who pressed upon both Eastern and Western Christianity. Like the rest, they were a challenge to both the soldiers and the missionaries. A century earlier, St Boniface had thought the conversion of the Slavs a task not worth undertaking. His successors had to think differently.

The troubled relationship between East and West was exacerbated not only by the Roman-Frankish fusion, but by Eastern iconoclasm, which was revived by each fresh Byzantine military disaster. Gradually, the split between Roman (or in the terminology we now use, Byzantine) East and barbarian West had led to a great cultural and political divide, that had been consecrated in 800 by the creation of what became the 'Holy Roman Empire' of the West.

In the ninth century, moreover, the Roman bishops began to develop what had at the beginning been a claim for seniority of apostolic tradition into a principle of legal jurisdiction. There had never been any question of the authority of the Roman bishopric as the bearer of doctrinal tradition that was connected with the apostles, Peter and Paul. To this was added the pope's importance as the guardian of the pilgrimage to the holiest of the churches and tombs of the Roman martyrs. In earlier centuries this authority and prestige were shared with those of the great apostolic eastern sees, to which had been added (by the agreement of church councils) the imperial see of Constantinople. The Muslim conquests made this balance of the ancient churches obsolete. Alexandria, Antioch and Jerusalem, and the now ancient cultural heritage of the Egyptian and Syrian churches (not to mention some of the other churches further to the east), had been as it were excised by a surgical operation.

The Pope and the Patriarch

Nicholas I (pope from 858–67) was also responsible for two critical episodes in the history of Roman relations with the East. The Byzantine Empire had by this time reorganized its military and administrative systems, and found ways, within its reduced boundaries, of more or less containing Muslim expansion. In 843, it had also at last settled the critical issue of iconoclasm in favour of restoring the veneration of the images. In principle, the way was open to a restoration of pacific

Below: A Carolingian ivory panel from c. 875 showing an archbishop amongst his choir.

Left: A pen, ink, wash and chalk drawing from the studio of Cesare Nebbia (1536–1613), called The Burning of Photius's Books and the Verdict on the Patriarch Photius. A former soldier and secretary, Photius became something of a pawn in the complex politics of Constantinople. He was twice made Patriarch but was finally exiled by Pope Leo in 886.

relations with the Western churches. But in practice this was not the direction things were to take. On the one hand, both Eastern and Western churches were sending missionaries to the Balkans and central Europe. On the other, the political distrust between the Franks and the Byzantines was very much alive.

The issue came to a head with the imposition by the Emperor (or more exactly, by his minister, the Emperor Michael III's uncle, Bardas) of a new Patriarch of Constantinople. This was because the existing Patriarch, the former learned layman and civil servant, Photius, himself the son of a former Emperor, had become unacceptable to the government. When the ousted Patriarch refused to accept exile and defeat, the Byzantine government called upon Pope Nicholas in Rome for support. This turned out to have been a bad political error. Nicholas sent legates to Constantinople, who recognized Photius as Patriarch, but were then repudiated by the pope who had sent them. Instead, Nicholas, on his own authority, removed Photius as Patriarch and restored the former incumbent, Ignatius. Photius replied by holding a council in Constantinople that anathematized and deposed Pope Nicholas in 867. The affair had turned into a direct confrontation between Eastern and Western churches.

The affair of Photius had direct consequence in the missionary field of Bulgaria. The khan of the Bulgarians had just accepted Christianity from Eastern Orthodox missionaries, but had subsequently become worried about the political consequences of his actions as they concerned the Byzantine Empire. He sent envoys to Rome, and offered acceptance of Western, Latin Christianity as an alternative. Pope Nicholas I agreed to the new arrangement with enthusiasm, although it did not lead in the end to the imposition of Western church allegiance on Bulgaria.

Rome and Byzantium Drift Apart

The missionary field in eastern Europe was not always dominated by a spirit of unthinking competition between Byzantium and Rome. The missionary brothers Cyril and Methodios, who more than anyone else were responsible for the conversion of the Slavs and their coming into possession of a written language for the transmission of the Gospel, were sent among the Slavs from Byzantium, but backed by Rome. Methodios was consecrated Archbishop of Pannonia by Pope Hadrian II, although political changes caused him to end (he died in 885) as Archbishop of Moravia. He was still in touch with Byzantium, and he has been called the last great figure of the universal church[2].

After the death of Methodios, relations between Rome and Byzantium were still not broken, especially as Byzantine rule in south Italy was vital to the defence of the peninsula against the Muslims. A change of dynasty in Constantinople, and the assembly in 869 of a council of Eastern bishops that endorsed the deposition of Photius desired by the popes, smoothed the way back to more normal relations between East and West. But the gap between the clergy of Rome and that of Constantinople grew wider every year. In Rome, a doctrine of papal primacy over other bishops that emphasized the magisterial jurisdiction of the Roman see was being formulated. The wholesale forgery of early church laws that backed up this sort of view (the 'Pseudo-Isidore' decretals, after a Spanish collection of church laws that had been wrongly attributed to the seventh-century clerk of that name) was carried out, not in Rome during this period, but in Francia.

The doctrine of Roman magisterial primacy supposed Roman supremacy over the Greek churches. Rome was very far, on this account, from forgetting that the Christian East existed. In the late ninth century, Greek ecclesiastical culture was still studied in Rome, and knowledge about it there was not

Left: The imperial crown of Charlemagne. It was used to crown Otto of Saxony in 960. As Holy Roman Emperor, Otto I based his rule on the pattern set by Charlemagne.

confined to a few Greek monasteries. The popes still wrote their letters on papyrus imported from the Greek-speaking world. There were learned men in the papal court such as Anastasius (once for a short time pope, but more important as the adviser of Pope Nicholas I) and his son Arsenius, who understood the theology and politics of the Eastern Church.

Papal Problems

The late ninth to the mid-tenth centuries were a particularly dark age for the Italian peninsula. The Frankish emperors, who made only occasional expeditions to Italy, were unable to protect the civilization of great churches and monasteries that their predecessors had set up there. Arab and 'wicked Christian' plunderers wandered in Italy where they willed. In Rome the military and political situation became desperate. The military aristocracy controlled and exploited the churches and their lands in Rome and elsewhere. The last great pope of the century, John VIII (872–82), was unable to stop them. The clerical leader of the one of the groups of powerful Roman nobles was Bishop Formosus of Porto, whose ambitions split Roman society in two, and caused anarchy in the city over a period of about thirty years. In 891 Formosus appeared to have triumphed by securing his own election as pope, and he died as pope in 896.

Such was the hatred he had occasioned that after his death his papal successor had the nine-month-old corpse of Formosus taken from the grave to be 'judged' by a synod of bishops. The corpse of the former pope was condemned, and his tenure of the papal office pronounced invalid. The fingers that had expressed benedictions were torn from the body, which was thrown into the Tiber.

Matters did not improve for the papacy after this sad scene. The factions of Roman nobles continued to control the papacy; in the first half of the tenth century the dominating family was that of the senator Theophylact. His daughter, Marozia, is second only to Lucrezia Borgia among the fabled bad women of papal history. It was claimed, perhaps falsely, that she was the mistress of Pope Sergius III (904–11), and the mother by him of the future Pope John XI (931–5). The 'prince and senator' Alberic, her son by her third marriage to a great prince of the Middle Kingdom, was certainly the ruler of Rome from 932 to his death in 954. Alberic's son, a worldly young cleric whose recreations were women, gambling and hunting, became Pope John XII in 955.

The Restoration of the Empire

In the tenth century the various Frankish dynasties that had succeeded to the regional supremacies of the former Frankish Empire became unrecognizable or extinct. The Frankish Empire was resurrected by a new German dynasty, that of the former Dukes of Saxony. The agent of this rebirth of an ancient concept was Otto of Saxony, who by marching to Italy in 960, and securing his coronation as emperor at the hands of Pope John XII, launched a new imperial rule that relied on the legal and tribal framework set up by Charlemagne over a century and a half earlier. Otto I had John XII deprived of the papal office in 963, after defeating the pope and his army.

In the East at this time, the Byzantine army was also undergoing one of its many rebirths, and was for the first time since the seventh century trying seriously, while still holding the Bulgarians at bay, to regain some of the frontiers lost to Islam. Under Otto I's immediate successors, an alliance of the Ottonian and the Byzantine Empires began to oppose the Muslims in southern Italy. But these military alliances did nothing for the cultural gap that now yawned between East and West. By the late tenth century the mental division had proceeded to a point where Liutprand of Cremona, a Lombard bishop of a north Italian see, sent as an envoy of the Emperor Otto I to Constantinople, found himself on arrival in the Byzantine capital – in spite of his supposedly privileged diplomatic position – an excluded and inferior foreigner, trying to move in an alien and hardly comprehensible world.

Otto I's grandson, Otto III, son of Otto II and of the Byzantine princess Theophanu, became Emperor on reaching so-called majority in 995; he was, however, still a youth of fifteen. He proved to be an antiquarian imperialist, who wanted to revive the Empire of Charlemagne, although in a form that resembled Byzantium more than Germany. He was the pupil of the Italian-born Greek teacher, Philagothos, and of the Frankish philosopher, Gerbert, the greatest clerical intellectual of his age, whom Otto made pope under the title of Silvester II (999–1003). The young Otto was deeply religious and deeply idealistic. He may have acquired from Gerbert some kind of eschatological premonition of the approaching end of the world, which may even have been connected with the millennium year through which he lived. He dreamed of the 'restoration of the Roman Empire'. He had the body of Charlemagne (who had died in 814) exhumed in Aachen, and took relics from the tomb. He took up residence in Rome, built a new palace on the Aventine hill, and lived there in the style of a Byzantine Emperor, with court officials who boasted sonorous Greek titles. When he returned to Rome for the last time in July of the year 1000, he was greeted not by the approaching horsemen of the apocalypse, but by the cavalry of Italian rebels, whom he had failed to subdue before his death near Rome in 1002.

1 Robert Hillenbrand, *Islamic Architecture: Form, Function and Meaning* (Edinburgh, 1994)

2 A. P. Vlasto, *The Entry of the Slavs into Christendom: an Introduction to the History of the Medieval Slavs* (Cambridge, 1970), p. 80

10

FROM PEACEKEEPING TO HOLY WAR

There had never been, during the first thousand years of the existence of the religion, any real question of making the Christian society into a pacifist society. That Christians wanted a pacific society was another, and a quite different question: there have been difficulties in obtaining such a society, which continue to plague us today. Christianity had taken shape in a Roman Empire whose military principles the Christians had from the beginning avoided calling into question.

The absorption of Christianity by barbarian societies revived the military questions in a different form. These societies were run by military aristocracies that in many cases attributed their ancestry to pagan war gods. Similar claims had been made by Roman Emperors; such things could be concealed or glossed over. But, because of the wide diffusion of power among the barbarian magnates, their military aristocracies were never controlled by the central authority in the way that the army was controlled in the Roman Empire.

Like the Christian Empire, the barbarian kingdoms were quite willing to exempt the ordained clergy from personal military service. But, because of the devolution of landed power in the early medieval West, it was going to be hard to separate the Church in a definite manner from the military organization of the kingdoms. The endowment of bishoprics and monasteries with huge grants of lands, inevitable in a gift-giving society, took the church lands out of the direct control of the nobles, but it did not remove them from noble influence entirely. The great nobles remained linked to the churches endowed by their families by a system of patronage that did not amount to ownership, but retained strong proprietorial characteristics. Nor did the king renounce his military rights over church lands.

The military crises of the ninth and tenth centuries, when Christian rulers were trying desperately to respond to the external threats of pagan raiders, much increased the pressure on the churches to use their resources for the defence of the kingdoms. In the former east Frankish kingdom, now ruled by a line of Saxon kings, the problem was solved in a particularly definite way, assigning to

Left: Crusaders take Jerusalem.

each bishopric a large military quota that the churchmen had to fill in time of war. There had been changes in military methods, and the most effective fighting unit had become the heavily armed cavalryman, who used expensive armour, weaponry and transport and was highly trained. By the middle of the tenth century the Saxon royal army depended on the heavy cavalry supplied by the bishops, as the nucleus of its main fighting force. The 'knight', as he later came to be called, had come to dominate Western warfare, and the Church was intimately concerned in the way he was financed and organized. That did not make the clergy the only employers of the knights, far from it: the great nobles were all surrounded by followings of heavily-armed retainers whose numbers corresponded to their rank and resources.

Church Militant

The manner in which the Church was involved with the military system varied from one region to another. In Anglo-Saxon England the bishops did not normally supply troops on the same basis as happened in Germany, but they often had to contribute large sums to buying off the raiders. In west Francia the clergy sometimes raised troops, but not in the same way, nor in the same proportions, as in the Eastern Kingdom. It was a long-lived system, especially in Germany, where in the twelfth century each of the great bishops still headed retinues of up to several hundred knights, which the king could call out for the army. By that time a similar system obtained in Anglo-Norman England, although the proportion of church knights in the royal army was much lower. In central Italy, when an abbot of the monastery of St Benedict's foundation of Subiaco died in 1145, the monastery's chronicler recorded that he left the monastery 'in great prosperity, and full of well-equipped troops.'

In western Europe the military calling was a precarious and competitive one that did not encourage orderly behaviour. In the ninth-century German romance *Ruodlieb* the hero is advised not to ride down the standing corn of the peasants more than is necessary, and is told to billet himself on peasants who have old and ugly wives: the story of a fellow warrior who murdered his host to have his young wife follows. This kind of bullying by troops billeted on the local people was as old as military history. But the early medieval knightly class was guilty also of extorting and stealing goods and

Above: Offa, King of Mercia (757–796), founder of St Albans, which he is holding in his hand. Charlemagne considered Offa to be an equal.

money wherever they could find them. Churches were not in the least exempt for their depredations.

From the tenth century onwards the clergy tried to react, especially in south and north-west Francia, against this kind of lawlessness and oppression. On the one hand, big meetings of repentance were organized by the clergy, in which unlawful bloodshed and violence against unarmed persons were renounced by those who attended, and penance done or promised for what had occurred. At the same time the clergy began to sponsor what was in effect collective action to discourage bloodshed and

Left: A detail from the twelfth-century Westminster Psalter shows a crusading knight kneeling in prayer.

Right: Monks encouraging crusaders as they set off. The Church faced a dilemma in reconciling pacific principles with warfare but defined the Crusades as a holy war.

disorder, by taking new spaces of time into the realm of the holy. In the 'truces of God' the local warrior class undertook to renounce warfare on specified days and church feasts. From Wednesday evening until Monday morning, for example, could be a period during which they swore to abstain from violence, either for the purpose of extortion – even to seize pledges given under contract – or for that of taking vengeance. The 'truces of God' were enforceable by armed action on the part of the community, led by its church leaders, and this sometimes occurred. Such peacekeeping action could be viewed now as a species of 'holy war', although it was not so termed at the time.

The churchmen were not going to repudiate the huge property donations that gave them control of a very large part of the social and economic resources of north-west Europe. Nor, in spite of the moral ambiguities involved in giving bishops the administrative control and financial responsibility for keeping troops on permanent standby, were they going to repudiate this partial militarization of the Church. What they objected to was the political control exercised by kings and great nobles, that enabled them to use secular legal forms for 'investing' churchmen with their benefices. Even more, they objected to the possibility that these powerful laymen could actually sell the benefices. This is, after all, a situation perfectly familiar to attentive readers of Jane Austen's *Pride and Prejudice*, although Lady Catherine de Burgh did not require Mr Collins to keep troops in the parsonage.

Despite this, the upper clergy were not all obsessed by their own wealth, or if they were, they also reacted against it. There was in the eleventh century a drift towards the hermit life, but it was not

Above: A detail from the Bayeux Tapestry. In the centre Bishop Odo wields a club. The clergy were not allowed to be armed but a club was not defined as a weapon.

a flight to desert places of Western holy men, comparable to that of the Egyptian and Syrian hermits of six or seven centuries earlier. Solitariness in early medieval Europe was a quasi-organized affair, most of which took place within reach of the monasteries; isolated holy men were viewed with some suspicion, even as a possible cloak for heresy. The desire to live the hermit's life was still there, but it often ended with the foundation of a new religious group that formed some affiliation with an existing monastic order. It is no accident that the best-known hermit of the time, St Peter Damian, was one of the main influences of his day in striving to impose a new and more severe religious discipline.

The papal court underwent radical change in the mid-eleventh century. Socially, it had for two centuries been controlled by the Roman aristocracy: the efforts of the Ottonian Emperors to change this, in the second half of the tenth century, had been in vain. But in the mid-eleventh century the Emperors again intervened in the affairs of the Roman clergy, this time more effectively, although to their own ultimate detriment. In 1046 the Emperor Henry III deposed Italian claimants to the papacy whom he deemed corrupt, and replaced them by a series of German bishops, who occupied the papacy until 1058. The most important of these was Bishop Bruno of Toul, who occupied the papal throne as Pope Leo IX from 1049–54. His pontificate proved a central one, both in defining the new papal policy of reform, and in its effect on relations with the Eastern Church. Leo IX appointed reforming cardinals to the Roman court from the Middle Kingdom, including a clerk from Lorraine called Humbert of Moyenmoutier.

Schism

At this period theological difference between the Eastern and Western churches was perhaps more to do with cultural and linguistic matters, than with critical differences in the ways that either church thought about the divinity. In the Western Latin liturgy it had very gradually became customary to recite the Creed in a form that referred to the Holy Spirit as 'proceeding from the Father and the Son', instead of using the earlier form, used at Chalcedon in 451, that restricts itself to saying that the Spirit 'proceeds from the Father'. Behind this difference of usage there do not seem to have lain the long years of highly articulate theological dispute that lay behind the ancient differences of opinion about the divine and the human in the person of Christ. The difference about the 'filioque' ('[from the father'] and from the son') may reflect a diversity of mentality, but it seems to have owed its existence much more to liturgical habit than to anything else, and in any case its use only became universal in the West in the eleventh century.

The Patriarch of Constantinople at the time of Leo IX of Rome was Michael Cerularius, an active character who seems to have

Below: The reliquary of Henry II (973–1024). Henry was crowned Holy Roman Emperor in 1014. He donated lavish rewards to the Church to ensure that he kept political control in both secular and spiritual matters.

decided to open some of the long-standing questions about the unsatisfactory practices and beliefs of the Latin Church. His most provocative act, which would have had economic and political results, was to close the Latin churches in Constantinople. It was unfortunate that this period of activism in Constantinople should have coincided with a quite unconnected period of activism in Rome. In 1054 Humbert of Moyenmoutier, who was particularly interested in theories of papal supremacy in the Church, was dispatched to Constantinople at the head of a small mission of like-minded clerks, to protest against the actions of Cerularius. The papal envoys were German noblemen of great power and influence, and the attitudes of these insolent barbarians to the upper Byzantine clergy, who were themselves conscious of a cultural superiority that needed no discussion, were judged by the Patriarch to be extremely unsatisfactory. It was a situation that Westerners were one day to encounter in the imperial Chinese court.

Humbert of Moyenmoutier and his colleagues met with the refusal of the Byzantine clergy to give any hearing to their complaints, which were not restricted to the matter of the closed churches, but complained of hostile Byzantine propaganda against the Latins. They stated the basic papal jurisdictional claims, which were totally unacceptable to the Patriarch. The reply of the Western delegation was to enter the church of Haghia Sophia without warning, and to solemnly deposit on the high altar a bull of excommunication of the Patriarch of Constantinople: they then hurriedly left the city. The Emperor Constantine was worried by this turn of events, and not particularly pleased that Cerularius had allowed it to occur. However, he was unable either to moderate the Patriarch's attitude or conduct, or to stop him from holding, a short time later, a synod that anathematized the Roman see on account of the conduct of its legates. The mutual anathemas were not finally withdrawn until 1965, although many attempts were made to reach an accommodation in the later Middle Ages.

The 'Schism of 1054' was not a turning point of church history. Its precedents stretched back for many centuries, and it was far less decisive for the relations of Eastern and Western churches than things that were later to occur during the course of the Latin Crusades, above all the sack of Constantinople by the Latins in 1204. But it was, nevertheless, a flashpoint that cannot be ignored. It demonstrated the extent to which the Western churches were tending to become one Church under papal leadership, and that showed also the unacceptability of this phenomenon to the Church of the East.

The Reform Papacy

The aim of the main church movement of the eleventh century was institutional reform that sought to preserve existing church institutions, while purifying and sanctifying them. As it happened, the attainment of these aims was to cause the transformation of many of the chief clerical institutions of the time, notably the Roman bishopric itself. But the reformers had it most to heart that church offices, which existed to serve the people of God, should no longer be bought and sold, and that the hands of laymen, hands that had often been stained with blood, should no longer transmit to the clergy the tangible symbols of their office.

Below: The Palace of the Normans in Palermo, Sicily. The Nomans took over the city in 1072 after more than 200 years of Arab rule.

The clerical group that more than any other understood these things was that of the German clerks introduced into the Roman bishopric by the Emperor Henry III from 1046 onwards. They knew about them because they themselves belonged to the uppermost levels of the German nobility, and to the court circles that had hitherto profited by them. The struggle against 'simony', the sale of holy things (Acts 8:18) was to be the main concern of the Roman Church for the following half-century.

The contested symbolism of the feudal 'investiture' with his benefice of a clerk by a layman (usually by the handing over of a staff or of some other sign of property) gave the struggle its modern name of 'Investiture Contest'.

The main figure in the stand-off with the German monarchy that the Roman popes led in the last three decades of the eleventh century was an Italian clerk called Hildebrand who on election took the title of Pope Gregory VII (1073–85). To oppose armed resistance to the Salian King Henry IV (reigned 1056–1105) was a practically impossible task for a Roman bishop, who in spite of the great prestige of his see was materially no more than the first bishop of the Empire. Gregory's assets did not lie in his armies, which melted away whenever he really needed them, but in his moral stature and diplomatic skills. In 1077, at their meeting at Canossa in north-central Italy, where he forced the king to appear before him as a penitent, Gregory came near to success. But the understanding with Henry at Canossa proved illusory. At the end of his life Gregory saw Rome taken by Henry's army (and subsequently much more thoroughly sacked, by his own), while he himself went off to die in exile. However, he may be said to have gained his essential aims, even if the German monarchy only acknowledged this some thirty-seven years after his death.

The wars of the Investiture Contest, even if unsuccessful, changed the outlook and status of the Roman papacy in a decisive way. To achieve their aims the popes had had to mobilize armies to fight in holy wars: there had been an attempt to create a new 'militia of St Peter'. The popes were already the feudal sovereigns of the Normans of southern Italy, on whose support they had depended in the later stages of the contest. In one sense the popes were fighting to avoid finding themselves in the situation of the German bishops, who were also the army generals of the German king, but in another sense they had themselves accepted a sort of full militarization. The preceding transformations had been detectable in the social history of the papacy since

Right: Seljuk raqqa bowl showing two Seljuk horsemen.

© Oriental Museum, Durham University, UK/Bridgeman Art Library, London

the early tenth century, but from the close of the Investiture Contest the papal monarchy may be said to have become a feudal monarchy among the other feudal monarchies. It was, of course, many other things besides.

The consequences of that militarization were worked out in a most unexpected way at the end of the eleventh century. The Roman bishops were not disposed to revoke the anathema of 1054, any more than the Greeks were to revoke theirs. Equally, they were indisposed to forget a Byzantium that had been the legal sovereign of the Roman bishops for at least two and a half centuries, and an Eastern Church that theological memory could not disregard. Politically, although the Byzantines had been finally expelled from southern Italy by their mutinous mercenaries, the Normans, Byzantium continued to be a very important factor in the seapower and political balance of the Mediterranean and Adriatic Seas. Rome could not afford to neglect any of these things.

In the same decade that Gregory VII was confronting the German king at Canossa, the balance of power had turned against the Byzantines in Asia Minor in a manner that was in the end to prove decisive. The Turks had for two centuries been the most important element in Muslim military power, but until this point they had featured as slave military levies rather than as independent actors. The intake of Turkish military slaves was to continue for the rest of the Middle Ages, but in the eleventh Christian century the Turks were to acquire an independent dynasty that played a major role in the Muslim world.

Seljuk attack

The Seljuk branch of the Turks, led by Tughril Beg, conquered Baghdad. In 1056 Tughril was made Sultan and King of the East and West by the Caliph. Tughril, and after him his son Alp Arslan, led the Seljuks in a series of holy wars against Byzantium in Asia Minor. They found very little determined resistance, and raiding armies were able to march far into the the interior of Cappadocia. The Byzantine Emperor Romanus Diogenes took his main army into Armenia to challenge Alp Arslan, and met him in 1071 near Lake Van, at the Battle of Manzikert. It was a last, desperate throw; the Byzantine army had for years been starved of men and resources. At this battle the Emperor was taken, and the Byzantine army destroyed. The result was to open most of Asia Minor to Seljuk attack, and to lead to the occupation of huge areas in Anatolia (not to mention the Aegean coast) by Turkish leaders; in 1085 Antioch also fell.

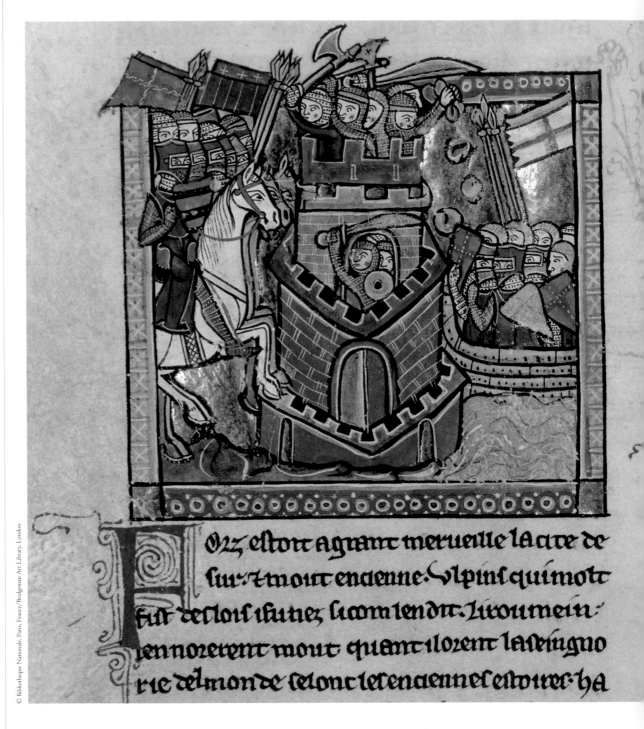

Right: The siege of Antioch from an illuminated manuscript. Antioch changed hands several times but in 1098 it was captured by the crusaders after a siege lasting six months.

The Byzantine experience with Norman mercenaries had been deeply disillusioning, and had ended, after the Battle of Manzikert, with the Normans themselves trying to set up their own principality in Asia Minor, but the Byzantines persisted in thinking that their own military incapacity might be offset by finding new sources of mercenary troops in western Europe. After 1081

Byzantium once more had an Emperor with a good military record and great talents as a diplomatist – Alexius Comnenus.

The sensitivity of the Roman bishop to what was happening in Eastern Christendom is known from a letter written by Gregory VII to a Burgundian noble in 1074, three years after Manzikert, in which the pope refers to the plight of the Eastern Christians in face of Saracen aggression. He says, very mysteriously, that if he resolves his own current military problems with the rebellion of his Norman feudatories, he may himself go to Constantinople to give armed aid to the Byzantines. Presumably, as he knew that Normans were already serving as Byzantine mercenaries in Asia Minor, he hoped either to bring those already in Byzantine territory back to obedience, or to take fresh contingents. The letter is interesting because it seems to show that armed voyages to the East which sound merely fanciful, were actually being contemplated in some way by the pope.

It is always tempting to modern people to think that because of their poor communications, medieval people were necessarily ignorant of what was happening in other cultures and at very great distances. The medieval poor were poorly informed, not surprisingly. But the Roman bishopric, recently energized by reforming zeal, also had traditional knowledge, and live diplomatic contacts that made it

Below: Peter the Hermit gives out crosses in support of the first Crusade. The image is taken from The History of Jerusalem from 1095 to its capture by the Christians, by the monk Robert. It was from the wearing of the cross that the Crusaders took their name.

*Right: The first Crusade. Crusaders consisted both
of organized armies and loose groups of peasants.*

the best observatory in western Europe of the Muslim and Byzantine Mediterranean. Over half a century earlier, another pope (Sergius IV) was said to have declared his wish to proceed himself to Palestine to succour the Christians there, after he had heard of the anti-Christian policies of the then Fatimid caliph. And in the very early years of the new reforming papacy, in 1064, the pope had specifically approved of the mustering of French warriors to fight against the Muslims in northern Spain.

There was another factor that made Western Christians of all sorts aware of the inner Islamic world. The pilgrimage to Jerusalem was one of the most persistent phenomena of the time. Pilgrims left from all over Christian Europe, from as far north as Scandinavia and Iceland, and from all over the north-west and the south, to make the risky and arduous voyage to Palestine. They made the voyage in groups that varied in size from a few dozen to several hundreds. Such pilgrimages were perfectly practicable throughout the century, except in exceptional circumstances of local wars or of anti-Christian riots. The pilgrims often included knights, even feudal rulers, who hoped to gain some more substantial hope of salvation, in spite of the constant bloodshed that marked their careers. The Muslim rulers of Palestine received them peaceably, partly because this was a profitable early-medieval version of long-distance tourism, but also because Islamic custom approved the grant of protected status to Christians or Jews who were thought not to harbour intentions of hurting Islam.

The Christian eleventh century also had its own versions of the expectation of the end of time. These have been present in the religion from the beginning. Prodigies, such as comets and reports of monsters, and disasters, such as plagues and famines, could affect such fears, and so also could the locally destructive results of wars. Reported happenings in Palestine and the East could also affect eschatological consciousness. The most important was the report of the 'destruction' of the church of the Holy Sepulchre in Jerusalem by the anti-Christian caliph, Hakim, that had been supposed to have disturbed Pope Sergius himself, in 1009. News of the Battle of Manzikert in 1071 must also have been disturbing. That unlearned people had much information of a political sort is unlikely. But some of the knightly class may have known such things.

There is also a kind of strange, but in appearance precise, geographical frame of reference in the Book of Revelation, that can make a no less powerful impression on the Christian consciousness than the strongly local Palestinian contexts of the Gospels. It must have been strange for anyone in the West to hear of the infidel seizure of Ephesus, Laodicaea, Philadelphia, Smyrna, that all figure in Revelation's geography.

Pope Urban II was elected in 1088, three years after the death of Gregory VII. At the time of his accession there was still a Church schism in force, that had resulted from the quarrels of the Investiture Contest. King Henry IV of Germany was still excommunicated, and most of his kingdom was in consequence outside the direct influence of the Gregorian obedience. Urban II was a Burgundian monk, from the great monastery of Cluny, which had been a formative influence on Church practice and thinking ever since its foundation in the early tenth century. He called a church council in the north-Italian city of Piacenza in 1095, that was attended by the ambassadors of the Byzantine Emperor Alexius. Almost certainly, the ambassadors asked for military help from the Western Christians against the Seljuk Turks in Anatolia, and emphasized the common cause of the Eastern and Western churches in the matter.

In Rome, Pope Urban II was still afflicted by the civil war that the schism had occasioned. He therefore did not return there, but from Piacenza travelled in the autumn of 1095 to Clermont, in the duchy of Aquitaine, in the south-east of Francia, to hold another church council. He perhaps

Suuc eston   *tiesme iour deleptembre eu*

Above: Armed knights and soldiers set sail for the first Crusade. Crusaders encompassed Christians of all ranks, including knights, many of whom hoped for material gain as well as eternal salvation.

preferred this area of Francia because King Philip I of France, whose lands lay elsewhere, was at the time under a cloud, as a result of his irregular relationship with Bertrade de Montfort. When the reform business of the council at Clermont was finished, Urban took advantage of the presence of so many of the bishops and nobles of southern France to go outside the walls of the town, where he could address a largely lay audience, and to make a statement and an appeal concerning the situation of Christians in the East.

The First Crusade

To a modern public accustomed to statesmen who address their audiences about events that have appeared on the television screens in the past few hours, the content of Urban's appeal may seem quite odd. The most recent event that he referred to was that of the fall of Antioch to the Muslims, which had happened ten years previously. He spoke of the desecration and defilement of other places by the infidel, although the events of which he spoke had started to occur after the Battle of Manzikert, twenty-eight years earlier.

Urban was the head of the Western Church at a time when the distinction between the lay and the clerical orders in Christianity was being emphasized by the reform party that he also headed. But he had just left the closed church council of bishops to talk to a gathering of laymen, some of them great noblemen, but for the most part knights. To these men, who were most of them soldiers, he talked without making distinctions of rank. He asked them, whether rich or poor, to put aside their quarrels (which he knew to be many) and to relent from their 'lawless persecutions', and to march to the East to the help of their fellow Christians. Urban offered his military ambience in 1095 a sort of battle cry: 'Deus le volt, it is the will of God.'

Urban had preached the first Crusade, though it had no name of that sort. The armed future pilgrims whom he wanted to send to the East had at Clermont torn up fabrics and marked them roughly with a cross to wear, hence *croisé* or cross-wearer. His argument for their departure contained, in fact, an implied judgement about feudal society. If he referred to their 'lawless persecutions' and their quarrels, he was repeating the protests that bishops in the middle and western kingdoms had been making for the past century, about the lawlessness and gangsterism of the knightly class. In wanting to despatch the lawbreakers across the eastern frontiers, he was trying to persuade them to voluntarily make a most arduous pilgrimage, a sort of holy exile. And, against all probability, the appeal worked. The probability was that he was despatching them to a harsh and terrible end in the unknown wilds of Anatolia and northern Syria.

There was, of course, a very large element of hard-headed political calculation in Urban's actions. The enterprise might have been conceived at Piacenza, while he was talking to the Byzantine envoys. He had probably at some stage entered into discussions with the leaders of the southern French nobility, who themselves had had some experience of fighting the Muslims south of the Pyrenees.

Above: Contemporary images portray the Jew as money lender in league with the Devil. Anti-Semitism flared during the period of the Crusades, giving rise to virulent propaganda.

© Lambeth Palace Library, London, UK/Bridgeman Art Library, London

Right: The Crusaders attacking and taking Jerusalem in 1099, when they massacred Christians and Jews. The image is taken from The story of Godfrey de Buillon and Saladin. Godfrey was elected Defender of the Sepulchre after the fall of Jerusalem.

In sponsoring a new holy war, Urban was not making a fresh theological departure that affected the theories of either Western or Eastern churchmen. For centuries, both Eastern and Western Christians had been encouraged to think that the faith could be either spread or defended by force of arms, and that God would look kindly upon those who died for the faith, even though in the East the clergy continued to look upon killing as sinful, no matter what the occasion. Where he was breaking fresh ground, was in supposing that a priest, acting as the minister of God, could propose and preach, and even (as subsequently became evident) to a limited extent control a holy war. He also incorporated in his actions at Clermont a statement that whoever went to Jerusalem on wholly religious grounds, not attracted by honour or money, but only to free God's Church, would have his whole pilgrimage accredited to him for forgiveness of sin, and would be free of all further penance. By this he invented what was in effect a new way to gain merit towards salvation. He also fixed Jerusalem as the object of the armed pilgrims.

It took two and a half years to assemble the forces that Urban had had in mind, for the expedition to Jerusalem. In the interim, two abortive popular expeditions had taken place, and it had also already become clear that one inevitable result of the preaching of the cross against the Muslims, was to stir up savage anti-Semitic riots and pogroms. The connection between Jerusalem and perfidious Jewry was too close in the Christian mind to avoid: even when, much earlier in the century,

the Shi'a Caliph Hakim had come down upon the Christians of Jerusalem, his actions had been attributed in the West to Jewish machinations.

The political disillusion that awaited the Byzantines, when the Western levies that they had asked for began to appear in Constantinople, was acute. It was not that the Byzantines were in the least ignorant about the Normans, who had, after all, stolen all the Byzantine possessions in Italy, and had attempted to set up their own dominion in Asia Minor, after the disaster of Manzikert. But, besides the perfidious Normans, the Western armies that arrived in Constantinople in 1097 included many of the greatest families of western Francia and the Middle Kingdom. They at first refused full feudal homage to Alexius, but oaths were found that satisfied both parties. The military co-operation that followed was real, and both sides were also conscious of the need for Christian unity. But distrust on both sides was real, too, and while the Westerners tended to think of the Easterners as other, barely acceptable Christians, the Easterners, following centuries-old habit, thought of the crusaders as barbarian auxiliaries.

Hardly any of the pilgrims in the Western armies that fought their way across Asia Minor in 1097 and 1098, in bitter and sometimes terrible conditions of exposure and hunger, had at the beginning any clear idea of what they were fighting for, beyond clearing their path to Jerusalem. But, like all holy warriors, they soon adopted the idea of armed martyrdom and holy vengeance. At one of the earliest battles, at Nicaea, their casualties 'all alike entered heaven in the robes of martyrdom, calling upon the blood shed in his name.' As the army marched on ruined roads over the anti-Taurus mountains in the

Left: A Islamic reliquary of the precious blood looted from the East.

autumn rains, many troops and whole baggage trains slipped over precipices, and the knights threw a lot of their heavy equipment after them. At the siege of Antioch (1097–8), an especially severe and terrible experience, accompanied by famine and ending in the religious frenzy that accompanied the finding of the Holy Lance, their determination was forged into a terrible instrument of war. The awful massacre of almost all the surviving combatants and non-combatants of either sex that ended the siege of Jerusalem in the summer of 1099 could have surprised no one who had accompanied the army. The Christian troops walked ankle-deep in blood in the streets, some of it Christian blood.

Below: Pieces from the shroud of St Josse acquired after the first Crusade. Many of the surviving Byzantine silk textiles were used in western graves to wrap the bones of a saint, revered ruler or bishop.

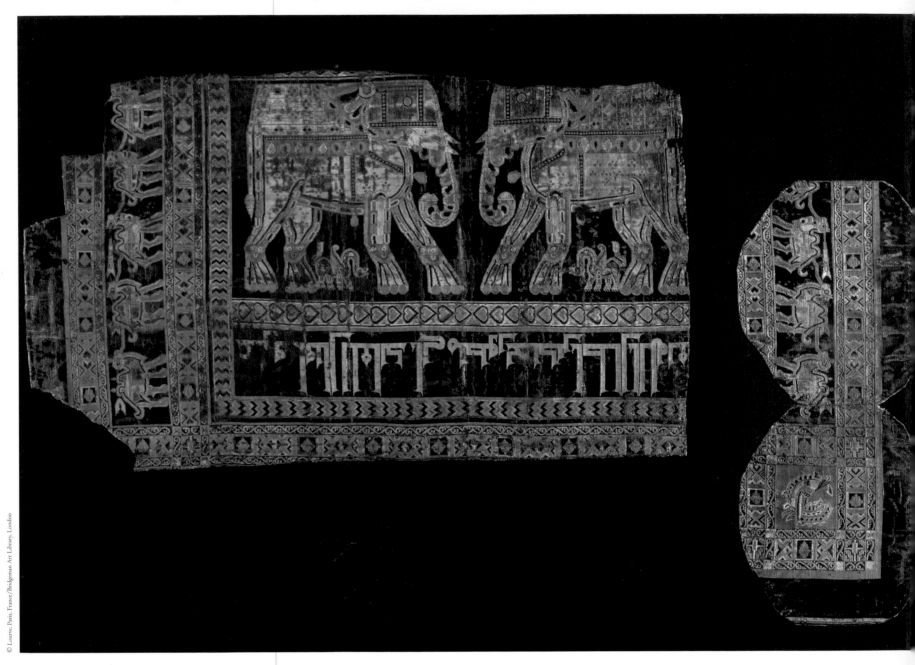

The establishment of the Kingdom of Jerusalem in 1100 went against the probable plans of Urban II (who by that time was dead). The earlier arrangement, under which Godfrey of Lorraine had been 'Advocate of the Holy Sepulchre' was much nearer to clerical desires, but almost certainly a clerical or papal patrimony of Palestine would have been impossible to run, and in the long perspective a grave embarrassment to the popes. This new frontier at the extreme edge of Christendom could only be given to feudal frontiersmen to defend, and the feudal Kingdom of Jerusalem, while in some respects a sickly plant, was probably about as healthy as any feudal kingdom set up under those desperate circumstances could have been expected to be.

Rather paradoxically, although the Latin Kingdom of Jerusalem had been the indirect result of the desire of the clergy to control the unruly and destructive feudal nobles, all it had really done was to transfer to Palestine many of those nobles, no less unruly and destructive than before, and to shift the moral and material burden of their finance, reinforcement and supply to the Western Church as a whole. This first experiment in Western collegiate colonialism, which is no surprise now to a West that has much experience in United Nations enterprises, was to have many unforeseen results for the Western Church, and particularly for the papacy.

The first Crusade was deeply significant both in the realm of faith and in the realm of power. The Eastern Church, in spite of any promises that had been made in Constantinople, was not restored in any part of the new Latin dominions: it was tolerated only under Latin control. Far from emerging as a great gesture of Christian solidarity, the Crusade had proved to be only one more act of betrayal of the eastern Empire by its Western mercenaries. In the domain of power politics, the Crusade was to herald a new period in the eastern Mediterranean in which Western seapower, mercantile and military interests were to be placed in a position in which they permanently retained the capacity to intervene. This was to continue even after the Crusader States had been pushed out of Syria-Palestine at the end of the thirteenth century. From the point of view of Byzantium and the Eastern Church, the Latin Crusade was a political death sentence, although one that took over a century to execute. From the point of view of the Roman papacy, the Crusade was the greatest political opportunity ever offered it in the high Middle Ages.

Below: A contemporary manuscript shows tormented souls locked in the jaws of Hell. It illustrates powerfully the fear of the apocalypse at the turn of the first Millennium.

Right: *Crusaders and Muslims battle against each other at the end of the first millennium.*

READING LIST

This reading list contains a few suggestions for people who would like to pursue some aspects of a huge and fascinating subject.

Chapters 1-3
E.P. Sanders, *The Historical Figure of Jesus* (Allen Lane-Penguin, London, 1993)
Geza Vermes, *Jesus the Jew* (2nd edn., SCM Press, London, 1983)
J. Murphy-O'Connor, *Paul: A Critical Life* (OUP, 1993)
W.H.C. Frend, *The Rise of Christianity* (Darton, Longman & Todd, London, 1984)
H. Chadwick, *The Early Church* (Penguin, 1967)
R. Lane-Fox, *Pagans and Christians in the Mediterranean World from the Second Century AD to the Conversion of Constantine* (Viking, Penguin, 1996)

Chapters 4-6
N.H. Baynes, *Constantine the Great and the Christian Church* (2nd edn., OUP, 1972)
T.D. Barnes, *Constantine and Eusebius* (Cambridge Mass., 1981)
Eusebius, *The History of the Church from Christ to Constantine* (trs. G.A. Williamson, Penguin, 1965)
P. Brown, *Augustine of Hippo: a biography* (Faber, London, 1967)
Saint Augustine, *Confessions* (trs. R.S. Pine-Coffin, Harmondsworth, 1967)
P. Brown, *The Rise of Western Christendom: Triumph and Diversity AD 200-1000* (Blackwell, OUP, 1997)
P. Brown, *The Body and Society: Men, Women and Sexual Renunciation in Early Christianity* (Faber, London & New York, 1988)
D. Knowles, *Christian Monasticism* (Weidenfeld & Nicholson, London, 1969)
Gregory of Tours, *The History of the Franks* (trs. L. Thorpe, Harmondsworth, 1974)
H. Mayr-Harting, *The Coming of Christianity to Anglo-Saxon England* (3rd edn., Batsford, London, 1991)
Bede, *Ecclesiastical History of the English People* (trs. R. Collins and J. McClure, OUP, 1994)

Chapters 7-10
A. H. Hourani, *A History of the Arab Peoples* (Faber, London, 1991)
M. Cook, *Muhammad* (OUP, 1983)
The Koran (trs. N.J. Dawood, Penguin, 1974)

INDEX